INSPIRATION

with

EXPLANATION

INSPIRATION
with
EXPLANATION

365 Life-Changing Goals

Jeffrey S. Brown

AVENTURA
PRESS

ISBN-13: 978-1-936936-10-6

Published by
Avventura Press
133 Handley St.
Eynon PA 18403-1305
www.avventurapress.com

First printing January 2017
Printed in the United States of America

FOREWORD

What I love most about Jeff Brown's writing is that it explains simply, how to live, how to be the best version of myself, and how to do what I was put here to do ... what we were ALL put here to do.

The difference between Jeff's writing and others that I have seen, is that it isn't over my head. His writing speaks directly to me, so that the only excuse I have if it doesn't change my life for the better, is that I didn't put it into practice. Everyone can understand it, and live it, the way that he explains it.

I was physically, mentally, and emotionally bankrupt and I tried absolutely everything to fix it ... but in the end, it was Jeff's help that finally brought me back to "Life." His teachings helped me overcome depression, anxiety, auto immune disorders, addiction, and any other problem that I could dream up... and now I actually look forward to the sun rising ever day so I can put each life-changing goal into practice and be free to live every second, of every day, to the fullest!

He writes what subconsciously, we ALL know that we should be doing, and to me, that's the beauty of Jeff's approach.

—Jennifer Coleman

Dedication

I am dedicating this, my first published work, specifically to a small handful of people whose encouragement and inspiration, made this project possible. I received help from so many, most of whom don't even know how much they helped me, because they thought I was helping them. So, to everyone that has asked for my help over the past 12-plus years... thank you! You have helped me, more than I could ever have helped you.

There are five people that I would like to thank very personally:

First, I would like to thank my parents. Charles and Glenda Brown are two of the most genuinely decent human beings that I have ever met... and they may never fully understand how much they have helped me, and everyone else they have ever come in contact with in this world. They are great parents to their four children! They are great grandparents! They were great children to their own parents! They are great siblings to their brothers and sisters! They are very simply all around great people! Most of my life I took these amazing people for granted, but now I can see they aren't like everybody else... they are exceptional! Mom... Dad... if I can manage to live even half as Right as you did... I will most certainly consider my life a success! Thank you... I love you!

Second, Eric and Christan Burnett... my two dearest friends. These two have mastered the art of giving freely of themselves to others. They help everyone they possibly can. They are stand up human beings, solid members of society, great parents, children, siblings, and friends! They never gave up on me... even when I had given up on myself. They were always there waiting to help me when I decided I was ready... and when push came to shove, it was this amazing couple that ultimately saved my life and then continued to help me rise from the ashes for many years afterward. I can never thank them enough for giving me the only Right kind of help there is in this world! The two of you are a beacon of hope, lighting the way for all who care to truly find their way in this world! Thank you... I love you!

Last, but certainly not least... my amazing fiancé. Jennifer Coleman has been a pillar of strength for me from the very first moment we met! It was this amazing woman that really made this dream a reality. I had been writing for about seven years, but I wasn't getting anywhere, as far as getting my work published. And when I was about to throw in the towel and accept the fact that my writing may never be anything more than a hobby, she decided to take matters into her own hands. With a little help from a friend, she took some of my writings, sat at her computer, printed, bound, and covered my first book from scratch, at her house and gave it to me as a Christmas gift. Seeing that book in print was absolutely the thing that inspired me to stand back up and follow this dream through! And if that wasn't enough... she was also the one that found, and put me in contact with my current publisher (Lee Sebastiani @ Avventura Press). Jennifer Lynn, you are beautiful... inside and out! You are an absolute inspiration! You are a spiritual power and presence in my life! You are my best friend, my soulmate, and the absolute love of my life! Everyone that reads this book, has YOU to thank for it! Thank you so much! You are a truly beautiful soul! I love you with my whole heart... and I will continue to do so for all time!

Introduction

"The most satisfactory years of your existence lie ahead"

—Anon.

I'm 43 years old. I have a 26-year-old son, and a nearly 6-year-old grandson. I'm a 3rd generation veteran; my grandfather was in the Army in WWII, my father was in the Airforce in Vietnam, and I was in the Navy in Desert Storm.

I've been around the world ... twice. I've been to Paris, London, Madrid. I've been to the top of the Eiffel Tower! I've sailed across the English Channel! I've been to Oktoberfest ... in Germany! I've been to Bourbon Street for Mardi Gras. I lived in Scotland for two years. I have owned a couple homes, a couple cars, and a couple businesses! I've seen and done more in my 43 years than most people could hope to see or do in two lifetimes.

I've experienced some major ups and downs along the way. I am a high school dropout who flunked out of 10th-grade English Lit ... but now I'm a published author. And I've done it all with a GED and without two nickels to rub together! It's been one hell of a ride so far and I'm certain that the next 43 years are going to be even more interesting than the first. I'm not one step closer to the grave, I'm one step closer to being truly alive!

I write because I got tired of reading poetic sophistries, with no practical application, that would temporarily inspire me, but never really change my life. I want to help you bring about a real and potentially permanent change for the better in your own life ... and the lives of others as well.

The beauty of the methods I employ is that they can be proven. Any philosophy of life is hard to prove on paper, but because I'm giving you the practical application, you can easily try my suggestions and prove to yourself, in your own heart, beyond the shadow of a doubt, whether or not they work. Don't knock it 'til you try it!

These writings are based in principle...and principles are infallible. These methods are tried and true! I have experienced them myself, and I have witnessed many, many others put them into practice as well. None of us practice them perfectly, but when we do in fact practice them, they work perfectly!

I have been living by and learning more about these principles for over a decade. When I properly applied them to everyday life, they raised my quality of life almost unimaginably!

If these simple, yet profound truths can have even half the effect on you that they have had on me... your life should be drastically improved.

Good luck ... and Godspeed!

—Jeffrey S. Brown

January 1

365 Great Days!

It's a new year, and on this day, new beginnings are in the forefront of everybody's mind. We all have hopes & aspirations that this year will be better than the last, and I have learned that the best way to make sure that I have a good year is to first make sure that I have a great day! My friend Kathy always says, "We can do anything for just one day," and I agree! The goal for today: Try to make a new beginning out of each and every day ... 365 great days would add up to one hell of a year! Have a great day, everybody!

Right ... Or Truth

"The scientist who refused to perform a certain experiment lest it prove his pet theory wrong"

I used to take great pride in being "right." So much so, that I would be willing to ignore some of the facts if they proved me wrong. Now I don't care who is right and who is wrong—I just want to know the Truth. The goal for today: Choose between being a slave to the need to be right ... or living a life of Happiness, Peace, and Freedom by knowing the Truth! Have a great day, everybody!

My Own Inventory

I once pointed out to someone what he was doing wrong and he said, "How about you take your inventory and I'll take mine?" I learned a few valuable lessons from this:

1. People don't like it when you point out their mistakes.

2. I shouldn't try to help people who aren't asking for my help.

3. The only actions that I need to be concerned with are my own.

The goal for today: Only help the willing ... and take my own inventory. Have a great day, everybody!

January 4

Claim What Is Rightfully Yours

"There is such a thing as taking the Kingdom of Heaven by storm." —Emmet Fox.

The storms of life can strike at any moment, at any point in time ... but so can Happiness, Peace and Freedom! The goal for today: Don't wait another minute to claim what is Rightfully mine ... a life more abundant! Have a great day, everybody!

No Better... No Worse

The best way to avoid feeling insulted is to know the Truth, and the Truth is ... we are all *smart* people, who sometimes do stupid things. We are all *good* people, who sometimes do bad things. We are all *honest* people, who sometimes do dishonest things. This is great news! Now I can stop judging other people ... and I can stop letting the judgment of others negatively affect me. The goal for today: Remember that I am no better, or worse, than anybody else. Have a great day, everybody!

January 6

Watch Them Stand Forever

Any and all successful problem solving starts with an Honest desire to fix the problem. This is more important than we think. *Knowing* won't fix it, *need* won't fix it, *fear* won't fix it ... but an Honest desire will. Example: A doctor *tells* me to quit smoking. I know I should quit. I need to quit. Fear is telling me to quit, yet I keep smoking. WHY!? Because the Honest desire isn't there. I don't really want to stop. The goal for today: Build my solutions on the bedrock foundation of an Honest desire and watch them stand forever! Have a great day, everybody!

Think … or Know?

Should I do what I think is right in my head, or what I know is Right in my heart? It's my brain's job to rationalize my decisions, right, wrong or otherwise; I can make terrible decisions, and somehow, my mind can justify them and make them sound perfectly sane and logical. It's my heart's job to tell me the Truth; I can never make bad decisions, do the wrong thing and feel good about it. The goal for today: Remember that I *think* with my head, but I *know* with my heart … and follow the Right One! Have a great day, everybody!

Take Action ... Get Proof

"Don't take my word for it ... try it and prove to yourself whether or not it's true." —Emmet Fox

There is a very fine line between being open-minded and being blindly led. I have to be open-minded to let an idea in, but proof comes from doing. Example: One person told me to "look out for number one"... and another person told me to "put the welfare of others first." They can't both be right and the best way to find the Truth is to try it. The selfish life made me miserable; the selfless life made me happy. The goal for today: Take action, get my proof, and be happy! Have a great day, everybody!

Respectfully Factual

"A house divided against itself cannot stand."
—Abraham Lincoln

This is a Principle, and therefore, it applies to everyone and everything. If division is the cause of our fall, there can be only one solution: Unity. How do we achieve Unity? By discovering these Principles that govern us all, instead of arguing about opinions that only apply to some. The goal for today: Watch Unity grow through true tolerance! I will respect your opinion... but live by our Principles! Have a great day, everybody!

January 10

Be Exceptional

I believe that what makes people exceptional is their ability to do the things of everyday life well. If I help others more than I help myself, that's exceptional! If I Love more than I hate, that's exceptional! If I'm Honest more than dishonest, that's exceptional! If my motives are based on Purity rather than fear, that's exceptional! I'm going to stop looking for world leaders and miracle workers ... and start being one! The goal for today: Be exceptional! Have a great day, everybody!

Anyone Can Pretend

For many years, I lived under the delusion that I could do what I knew in my heart was wrong, and still be happy. I'm not talking about those moments where I forget that I'm an ass and pretend to be happy. I'm looking for those moments when I can look into my own eyes and the eyes of others and honestly say to myself that I'm the best person I know how to be today. The goal for today: Don't pretend to be happy. Be a good person and be *genuinely* happy! Have a great day, everybody!

What Life Is All About

I thought that living the Right way would be boring. I was afraid to believe in God. I was afraid to be a good person. I was afraid to show compassion ... because I was afraid of what others might think of me. Now I know that living the Right way is far more interesting, exciting and fulfilling than I ever could have imagined. The goal for today: I'm going to pray. I'm going to do what's Right. I'm going to Love and help people and I'm going to enjoy the hell out of it ... 'cause that's what Life is all about! Have a great day, everybody!

Find and Live by Facts

At thirty-two years old, I was at a dangerous crossroads in my life and I honestly didn't know if I was going to make it through. When I went out in search of a solution, all I kept hearing was "in my opinion" ... "in my opinion" ... "in my opinion." And every time I heard it, I walked away and looked elsewhere. Finally, someone said, "I have a fact-based solution" and I jumped all over it. With my life on the line, I couldn't risk going off of opinions. The goal for today: Keep my opinion to myself, disregard *your* opinion, and put the work into finding and living by the facts! Have a great day, everybody!

A Know It All That Knows Nothing

Did you ever believe something wholeheartedly and later found out that you were wrong? If so, were you able to admit it? A lack of humility can be dangerous. Preconceived ideas, stubbornness, and the fear of admitting when I'm wrong are three things that are guaranteed to keep me from the Truth. Not only will humility help me find the Truth, but it will encourage others to do the same and we won't live in a world full of know-it-alls that know nothing. The goal for today: Humility! Have a great day, everybody!

Eliminate Fear

Peace of mind can be a difficult thing to acquire and an even more difficult thing to hang on to. The only way to achieve Peace of mind is by overcoming fear. I must correct the fear of the past (depression), and I must live in the present to avoid the fear of the future (anxiety). The goal for today: Find out what I'm afraid of and eliminate it. Do whatever it takes to keep it that way and enjoy Peace of Mind! Have a great day, everybody!

Change for the Better ... Or the Worse

Change—an inevitable law of life! Most of us fear change, and that fear sometimes causes us to turn away things that might be good for us. Not all change is good, but to refuse to change is always bad. Change will happen whether we like it or not, so it makes more sense to bring about and embrace the change that we want rather than fight against it and end up with some change that we *don't* want. The goal for today: Embrace good change to ensure that bad change doesn't steamroll us. Have a great day, everybody!

⇌

And Be Free

We are all unique. We are all different in our own little ways. However, there are two things that are identical in every human being in the history of mankind: 1) Every human problem that has ever taken place was the result of an individual's being resentful, selfish, dishonest and afraid. 2) Every human problem that has ever been solved has been solved by an individual's being Loving, Selfless, Honest and Pure. The goal for today: Learn how to spot, admit and correct those four things and be free! Have a great day, everybody!

January 18

We Are All Good Enough

Self-esteem—*that's* what we are lacking! A lack of self-esteem ... being afraid that I'm not good enough, strong enough, smart enough, attractive enough ... that causes all of my problems and it's not even real. The only reason people would tell me that I'm not good enough is because they have no self-esteem. And if I believe them, then I have no self-esteem, and this problem is spreading like a disease in this world! The goal for today: Know that we are ALL good enough. Don't try to bring others down, and don't let others bring me down! Have a great day, everybody!

January 19

Let Good Move You

Every once in a while I see or hear something that is so inspiring that it moves me to tears. It makes me feel alive. It reminds me that we're here for a reason ... and that reason is to learn how to Love each other! Right after this uplifting feeling, I wonder why the world isn't living this way. Then I remember that it's not my job to police the world, it's my job to make sure that I am living this way. The goal for today: Do my part. Do what's Right. Love everyone. Live Life. Let that feeling that moves me be who I am today! Have a great day, everybody!

http://youtu.be/pK2WJd5bXFg

January 20

Love Freely

We are all born knowing Right from wrong and we are all born with the Free will to choose which one we will partake in. I believe that we exist to learn how to use our Free will to Love and help each other. We live in a world today that is trying to force us to care about each other and when I'm forced against my will to Love someone, then it isn't Love at all ... it's coercion. I can learn, grow and prosper by Loving because I WANT to, or I can live in ignorance, shrink and fail at life by loving because I HAVE to. The goal for today: Love Freely! Have a great day, everybody!

Don't Complicate It

I once had a problem that I literally spent a good twenty minutes trying to explain to a friend and when I was finished rambling through a million minor details, he said, "Oh, so you were thinking about yourself too much." And I thought ... could it be that simple? The goal for today: Stop complicating my problems. They are all caused by being selfish, resentful, dishonest and afraid. Then I can stop complicating the solutions as well, which are all found by being Selfless, Loving, Honest and Pure! Have a great day, everybody!

January 22

Think Right, Sleep Right

I used to have a hard time sleeping, but once I figured out why, I was able to fix it. I didn't sleep because of my thinking. It didn't matter if I was thinking about the past, the future, or the weather—my brain wouldn't let me rest. One night I put my head on my pillow and asked God to help me sleep and this is what He said: "It's important to think about these things... but not now." We can't turn our brains off, but we can point them in the Right direction. The goal for today: Focus on the task at hand! Have a great day, everybody

JANUARY 23

In That Order

Spiritual, Mental, Physical ... in that order. The Truth comes from my heart, then my mind decides whether to accept it, or reject it, then the body blindly follows. The mistake that I made most of my life was that I thought the physical came first. I thought if I changed people, places and things, then I would be at peace. I was wrong! The heart is where Peace originates and once my mind accepts that, my life will start to change for the better. The goal for today: Look inside for real Peace! Have a great day, everybody!

Tell It Like It Is

"You can talk about hopelessness because you offer a solution."

I used to pat people on the back and tell them "Everything's going to be OK," even if it *wasn't* going to be OK. I did it because the alternative was to say "You're screwed, and I don't know how to help you." Well, I have finally learned how to solve problems—a lot of problems, and now I can confidently say to people "This is bad ... but there is a solution." The goal for today: Tell it like it is, but make sure I know what it is first! Have a great day, everybody!

Fact or Opinion?

A friend: Porn is immoral, right?

Me: Why do you think it's immoral?

A friend: Because it's selfish.

Me: Selfishness is definitely immoral.

Whether or not porn is immoral is an opinion. Whether or not selfishness is immoral is a fact. These four things are ALWAYS wrong: selfishness, resentment, dishonesty and fear ... everything else is circumstantial. If this idea could be accurately conveyed to the world, it would literally solve ALL of our problems. The goal for today: Know the difference between Fact and opinion! Have a great day, everybody!

We're Why

I believe that God has a plan. He wants us to be happy, as the result of learning how to Love each other. Only one thing can spoil that plan, and that's us. Human beings, with free will, have been throwing a wrench in God's plan since the dawn of man. When something goes wrong, we ask "Why would God do that?" or "Why would God let this happen?" when we should be asking "What part of God's plan did we screw up?" The goal for today: Line my will up with God's will and be happy! Have a great day, everybody!

Real Love

Sincerity is grossly undervalued in the world today! We think that as long as we don't break the law, we've done enough ... and that simply isn't true. Example: The Bible says "Thou shall not kill," but did you know that it also says the only way to sincerely achieve that goal is to rid our hearts and minds of hate and anger (Matthew 5:21/22)? Loving my neighbor by force of law may keep me out of jail, but it won't get me into Heaven—that requires real Love! The goal for today: sincerity! Have a great day, everybody!

A Better Understanding

This is what I mean when I use these words:
God = The innate ability to know Right from wrong.
Heaven = The good feeling that comes from doing the Right thing.
Bible = Principle based instruction manual (with a few dangerous opinions sprinkled around in it).
Love = Impersonal sense of good will toward all.

I'm not saying that anyone has to agree with them. I just thought I'd throw this out there to add a little clarity to my messages. The goal for today: Talk about things like God so we can better understand each other! Have a great day, everybody!

"C" Is the Right Answer

What's the Right thing to do when I make a mistake?

A. Pretend it didn't happen and hope no one finds out.

B. Deny it and tell a series of elaborate lies instead.

C. Admit it and put an honest effort into correcting it.

I have tried all three and I can say, beyond the shadow of a doubt, that 'C' is the one that works best. I once read that "The Truth always heals,"and I have found that to be entirely accurate. Once I admit my mistakes, all the sick and stressful feelings go away. The solutions become clearer and people are usually willing to help. The goal for today: Admit my mistakes and help others fix theirs! Have a great day, everybody!

Your Anger Takes Away Your Peace

Anger destroys peace. Not the peace of the other person, but the peace of the person that is angry. There have been times when the person I was angry at didn't even know I was angry and therefore, the only person that suffered as a result of my anger was me. I once read that harboring resentment is like me drinking poison, thinking that the other person will die from it. All we accomplish with anger is the poisoning of our own souls. The goal for today: Eliminate anger with Love! Have a great day, everybody!

Real Freedom

Yesterday, a friend associated the word *Free* with the word *Happy*. This is really a profound realization! The Declaration of Independence says that we are Free to pursue Happiness, but once you actually attain Happiness, the word Free takes on a whole new meaning. A lot of people are free in the respect that they are not physically locked in a cage, but real Freedom = Happiness. The goal for today: Don't stop at physical freedom. Press on to Happiness and feel what it's like to be Truly Free from the inside out! Have a great day, everybody!

FEBRUARY 1

A More Genuine Life

I used to manipulate people into loving me. I used to give, expecting something in return. I used to use "my truth" as an excuse to do wrong. I used to base all of my decisions on fear. Through that misery, here is what I learned: Love must be a choice ... or it isn't really Love. Selfless acts must have no strings attached ... or they are not really selfless. Honesty must apply to us all ... or it isn't really honesty. Pure motives must bring good ... or they are not really pure. The goal for today: Live a more genuine life! Have a great day, everybody!

Humility and Helpfulness

"I can't escape this now, unless you show me how."
—Imagine Dragons

I ran into a problem that I didn't know how to fix, and I was afraid to ask for help. I thought that needing help was a sign of weakness, but it's not. It's just an admission that I don't know everything. It doesn't make me weak or stupid, it makes me humble and that's a good thing. Once I asked for help, not only was I able to solve my problem, but I also had the power to help others solve their problems. The goal for today: humility and helpfulness! Have a great day, everybody!

February 3

Forgive and Fix Fears

If someone wrongs me and I feel hurt, I've got two problems that need to be addressed. I have to forgive in order to get rid of my resentment … but I also have to find the fear that caused me to feel hurt and address that part of the problem too. Forgiving their actions won't make my fear go away and that's where my hurt comes from. The goal for today: Remember that healing is a two part process: 1) Forgive the wrong doings of others and set them free. 2) Find and fix my own fears and set myself free! Have a great day, everybody!

FEBRUARY 4

It Knows Best

"The light which shines in the eye is really the light of the heart. The light which fills the heart is really the light of God." —Rumi

One day I looked into my own eyes in the mirror and told myself a lie, but I found it impossible to convince myself of this lie. The reason that I couldn't convince myself is because they are not only my eyes, they are God's eyes and there's no fooling God.—I've tried. The goal for today: Get in touch with the Truth that comes from within and listen to It—It knows best! Have a great day, everybody!

FEBRUARY 5

Our Side

My side, your side, and the Truth! You shouldn't blindly follow me and I shouldn't blindly follow you. We should listen to each other, study our history, analyze the facts and work together to reestablish the Truth. I say "reestablish" because the Truth never leaves us ... we simply turn a blind eye to it. The goal for today: Screw my side. Screw your side. Let's find the Truth and call it our side! Have a great day, everybody!

Tact

"Tact is the art of making a point ... without making an enemy." —Johan Wolfgang Von Goethe

When I make a point using a mistake as the example, I try to point out my mistakes, not yours. When I make a point using a victory as the example, I try to point out your victories, not mine. If I point out your mistakes, it will probably upset you, and the point will be lost. If I point out my victories, you'll view me as arrogant, and the point will be lost. The goal for today: Practice tact and common sense so I can reach and help more people. Have a great day, everybody!

My Fear ... Not Your Actions

If I get mad, I try to look at myself, not the person that I think made me mad. Example: If someone cheats on me and I get mad, it's because I have a fear of being alone. If someone is talking bad about me and I get mad, it's because I have a fear of public opinion. If someone steals from me and I get mad, it's because I have a fear of running out of money. So you see, my anger is actually caused by my fear—not your actions. The goal for today: Get rid of fear ... and live free of anger! Have a great day, everybody!

FEBRUARY 8

Enjoy Life

"We absolutely insist on enjoying life."

Today, I will not let others dictate my mood. I will not let others steal my peace. I will not let anyone or anything bring me down. Today, I will hold my head up. I will know who I am. I will be happy. I will Love. I will help people. I will be the best person I know how to be. Today: I will absolutely insist on enjoying life! Have a great day, everybody!

~

Change Inside

A few years ago my life was falling apart. I was miserably unhappy and my first thought was "I need to get out of this town and away from these people." And much to my dismay, I was still miserably unhappy when I moved to a new town with new people. The reason that moving didn't work is because the problem was inside of me, and until something changed inside, the problem could not be solved. The goal for today: If I'm not happy with my life, the first thing I should change is ME! Have a great day ,everybody!

Get Off the Roller Coaster

I lived most of my life on an emotional roller coaster and it was exhausting ... dizzying. When I went out in search of a solution, this is what I found: I had to stop taking everything so personally—it's not always all about me. I had to stop lying to myself about my worth, my strength, and my responsibilities. I had to stop blaming my highs and lows on everyone else. I had to stop basing my decisions on fear. The goal for today: Learn how to cope with life and get off the roller coaster! Have a great day, everybody!

Set My Boundaries, Not Yours

"Their faults are not discussed. We stick to our own."

I once thought, "My girlfriend made me defensive and I need to tell her about it and set some boundaries." This is an absolutely terrible idea! 1) It's a lie to believe she "made"me defensive, as if I had no choice in the matter. 2) If I say that, I can guarantee that she will become defensive. 3) The best way to get people to see their mistakes, is to admit my own. The goal for today: Don't be a doormat, but don't treat others like one either! Have a great day, everybody!

Loving, Disciplined, and Confident

If I want to overcome the fear of being alone and have a happy, healthy relationship, I must focus on giving Love, rather than getting Love. If I want to overcome the fear of running out of money, I must be disciplined and get rid of the desire to spend more than I make. If I want to overcome the fear of what others think of me, I must find out who I am and learn to be the best version of myself that I can be. The goal for today: Know that Happiness doesn't come from women, money and popularity. It comes from being Loving, disciplined and confident! Have a great day, everybody!

FEBRUARY 13

Help the Willing ... Pray for the Unwilling

Sometimes I know what's best for people, sometimes I don't. Either way, I have no right to force my will on other people. I can help only the willing and when I attempt to help the unwilling, I usually end up doing more harm than good. For example: I've learned a lot about the nature of God, politics and addiction, but I have no right to force you to believe what I believe—even when I'm right! The goal for today: Help those who are asking for help and allow the rest the freedom to follow their own beliefs! Have a great day, everybody!

Understand and Love

"It's impossible to understand someone and not love them." —Ender Wiggin

If I understand that most people lie because they don't know the Truth, then I won't be hurt by their lies and I can Love them. If I understand that people are hurtful because they have been hurt, then I won't get angry and I can Love them. If I understand that most arrogance comes from a lack of self-esteem, then I won't become fearful and I can Love them. The goal for today: Don't take it personally—understand and Love! Have a great day, everybody!

Wisdom Is Born of Experience

There is Wisdom in all things! If I'm looking hard enough, I can learn from every person and experience. If I'm told the Truth, I should learn from it. If I'm told a lie, I should learn from it. If someone helps me, I should learn from it. If someone hurts me, I should learn from it. We are all surrounded by lessons on all sides at all times ... and the bad ones are just as important as the good ones. The goal for today: Be grateful for every experience—good, bad or otherwise—because Wisdom is born of experience! Have a great day, everybody!

~

Same Problem ... Same Solution

I look at human problems the same way I look at math problems. I believe that 2+2=4. If I give you the same problem, do you come up with a different solution? Now this: (Problem) self-ishness = unhappiness. (Solution) selflessness = happiness. If we have the same problem, we MUST have the same solution. The goal for today: Know that we all have the same problems and the same solutions. Then we can truly Live together and Love each other! Have a great day, everybody!

What You Believe

When people comes to me with a problem, it's not my job to tell them what's right or what's wrong. It's my job to ask them "Do YOU think it's selfish, resentful, dishonest or afraid?" I teach people how to consult their own conscience rather than give them my opinion. You will act on what YOU believe, not what I believe ... and misery comes from trying to live up to other people's standards. The goal for today: Help people find their own answers, because the Right answers always come from within! Have a great day, everybody!

Don't Let Fear Keep You From Doing It

Being nervous is different from acting on fear. We all get nervous from time to time. It's when we allow that fear to govern our actions that we have problems. Example: One of my biggest fears was public speaking, and I let that fear get the best of me for years. I have finally overcome that fear. I still get a little twinge of nervousness, but I don't let that keep me from doing it and the more I practice it, the easier it gets. The goal for today: Destroy fear with thoughts of Faith and Freedom! Have a great day, everybody!

My Fault ... Not Yours

It's not OK for me to have a bad day and take it out on someone else. I did things like that for years. I would treat you like garbage ... feel bad about it ... and then justify it by saying "I'm sorry, I'm just having a bad day." First of all, I do believe that happiness is a choice and if I'm having a bad day it's my fault, not yours. Next—it's never OK for me to treat people poorly, even if they have actually wronged me, because resentment is destructive. The goal for today: Don't have a bad day to begin with, but if I do, I should keep it to myself! Have a great day, everybody!

Live Free of Anger and Fear

We can learn from every experience. My neighbor is mad at me. Every time I see him, I smile, wave and say hello and he snarls, turns his head and snubs me. I don't know why, but I know I didn't do anything wrong, so I'm not too worried about it. This experience has taught me two very valuable lessons: 1) Anger hurts angry people more than the person they're angry at. 2) If I'm not doing anything wrong, I don't care what other people think of me. The goal for today: Live free of anger and fear! Have a great day, everybody!

Honestly Seek, Unselfishly Ask, Unconditionally Love

If I could prove to you, beyond the shadow of a doubt, that God exists, would you want me to? Most of my life I would have answered "No." Once I decided that I did want to find God, all I had to do was honestly seek. If I wanted or needed something from Him, all I had to do was unselfishly ask. If I wanted to feel loved, all I had to do was unconditionally Love. If I wanted to be Free, all I needed to do was what I knew in my heart was Right. The goal for today: Know the Truth and live it ... by giving Love! Have a great day, everybody!

Strive for Perfection

The key to living a perfectly happy, healthy, useful, productive life is to be 100% Selfless, Honest, Pure and Loving. I'm not perfect, but it's not because I don't know how to be. I guess my point is this: Even though I still make mistakes, I'm no longer confused about how it happened and if I know what caused it, I can fix it. If I'm not happy, healthy, useful and productive, I simply need to be more Selfless, Honest, Pure and Loving. The goal for today: Strive for perfection and grow happier every day! Have a great day, everybody!

⌐

Happy = Right

Do you want to be right ... or do you want to be happy? I like this little saying and after a few years of trying to practice and understand it, here is what I've learned: 1) Even if you are right about what you are arguing about, the fact that you are arguing about it makes you wrong. 2) There are some things that simply are not important enough to argue about. 3) There are some arguments that simply cannot be won. The goal for today: Remember that right doesn't always equal Right ... happy equals Right! Have a great day, everybody!

My Thoughts Don't Control Me

"Our constant thought of others and how we may help meet their needs."

Any time I feel sad, lonely, depressed or anxious, I want to think about how I can be helpful to someone else. If I sit and dwell on my bad feelings, they get worse. If I turn my thinking away from the negative to something positive and constructive, like helping others, those feelings are driven out. The goal for today: Stay positive and know that I control my thoughts and feelings—they don't control me! Have a great day, everybody!

Accountable for My Own Happiness

Yesterday, I talked about being in control of my own emotions and a friend pointed out what a powerful thing that can be. Knowing that I am in control of my thoughts, feelings and actions holds me accountable for my own happiness, or lack thereof—no more blaming others when things don't turn out right. But at the same time, it sets me free. I'm no longer at the mercy of the world around me. The goal for today: I will embrace accountability and responsibility in order to experience true Freedom! Have a great day, everybody!

Get a Positive Outcome

I can control my emotions by understanding how they work. I take a piece of information ... attach an emotion ... and get a physical outcome. Example: Someone calls me an idiot. I feel hurt. I hang my head and feel bad about myself. The first and last parts are out of my hands, but the middle, where I choose an emotion, is entirely up to me. If someone calls me an idiot, and I choose to be compassionate toward him or her, then the physical outcome will be Peace! The goal for today: Choose a positive emotion and get a positive outcome! Have a great day everybody!

FEBRUARY 27

Love ...Without Exception

Someone recently said to me, "I'm glad I don't have a 'Bad Side' anymore" and it made me smile. Anger ... resentment... hatred ... these are some of the most destructive forces on earth! We justify and defend our anger. We revel in it, as if it were a good thing. Sometimes we flat out love it and can't wait to spread it around and share it with others. IT'S GOT TO STOP! The goal for today: Love my family. Love my friends. Love my neighbors. Love my exes. Love my rivals. And Love my enemies! Love, without exception! Have a great day, everybody!

Work Hard ...Don't Live Hard

"Easier said than done." I say this to people a lot, but recently, I'm beginning to realize that it's only half true. Doing the Right thing is always easier than doing the wrong thing. The hard part is to understand what that means. Example: There is a big difference between earning what I get out of life and constantly struggling to survive. Putting the effort into living a good life is infinitely easier than trying to live a good life without putting the effort into it. The goal for today: Work hard ... and life won't be so hard! Have a great day, everybody!

March 1

The Paradox of Life

1. Helping others helps me.
2. Working at life makes life easier.
3. Fear of being alone will cause me to be alone.
4. Love is the only way to stop hate.
5. Admitting a lie will earn you trust.
6. Giving is the best way to get.
7. Forgiveness comes from forgiving.
8. Bullying, abuse and arrogance are caused by an inferiority complex.
9. The best way to make a first impression is to listen ... not talk.

The goal for today: Start putting others first and watch the paradox of life lead us to Happiness, Peace and Freedom! Have a great day, everybody!

MARCH 2

Happiness Is Necessary

"The joy of living we really have, even under pressure and difficulty."

This quote reminds me of my interpretation of the story of Job in the Bible. It's easy to be happy when everything is going my way. It's much harder, yet infinitely more important to still be happy when the shit hits the fan. Not only is happiness possible under difficult circumstances, but it's absolutely necessary in order to triumph over the difficulty. The goal for today: I'm going to be happy ... NO MATTER WHAT! Have a great day, everybody!

MARCH 3

Help or Enable?

Where is the fine line between giving freely and being taken advantage of? This is the
sixty-four-million-dollar question. The answer is simple, but there are many variables.
When giving stops feeling good, it's either because I'm being selfish, or I've gone too far. If
I'm being selfish, I should change my attitude
and get back to helping. If I've gone too far, I
should stop doing for people what they could
and should be doing for themselves. The goal
for today: Know my own heart so I can help
people the Right way and give without getting
hurt! Have a great day, everybody!

Change or Forgive

Sometimes you're mean to me because you're a jerk. Sometimes you're mean to me because *I'm* a jerk. It's never really OK to mistreat people, but that's not the point here. The point here is that it is vitally important for me to be honest with myself about my attitude and actions. Being ugly on the inside makes people not want to be nice to me. A bad attitude is a turn off to everyone. The goal for today: Honestly analyze the treatment I receive and if it's me, I will change—if it's you, I will forgive! Have a great day, everybody!

Nothing and No One

It's not my girl's fault if I'm unhappy. It's not the world's fault if I'm not at peace. It's not the government's fault if I'm not free. If these things are missing from my life, it's not their fault, it's my fault for depending on them for my supply. We all have a God-given right to these things, and these things never come from outside of us. The goal for today: Know that Happiness, Peace and Freedom come from inside, then nothing and no one can take them from me! Have a great day, everybody!

MARCH 6

Our Duty

When I was in the military I was taught that "I don't know" is an unacceptable answer and inaccurate information gets people killed. I remember thinking, "Damn... they just told me that I'm not allowed to not know." It was stressful at times, but I'm grateful for the experience and I still try to practice it. "I don't know" feels like a copout, and pretending to know feels like a lie. The goal for today: Find answers. Not because I'm a know-it-all, but because it's our duty as fellow human beings to help each other find those answers! Have a great day, everybody!

MARCH 7

~

Intuition

Sometimes the Right thing to do is to bend over backwards to help someone. Sometimes the Right thing to do is to not bend over backwards to help someone. And the only way to know which one is Right, in any given situation, is through our God-given intuition. If I'm paying attention, I can tell when people are genuinely trying to do what's Right ... and I can tell when they're not. The goal for today: Learn how to help the Right people ... the Right way ... for the Right reason! Have a great day, everybody!

Try It

Talking to a friend about the difference between a fact and an opinion, he said, "How do I know that what you're saying right now isn't just your opinion?" and the answer is simple ... try it. I was once told that I have to put myself first in order to be happy. I tried it. It didn't work and now I know the Truth. I have a fact. The Great Fact of Life is this: If I'm not happy at the end of the day, then I am doing something wrong. The goal for today: Let the outcome serve as proof of whether or not I did the Right thing! Have a great day, everybody!

Don't Just Refrain ... Change

I don't just bite my tongue or refrain from lashing out. I change how I feel. I'm at this strange place in life where I try to be patient, tolerant, kind and loving toward everyone—not because I have to be, but because I want to be. If I feel the need to lash out, it's because there is something wrong with me, not you. If I allow your actions to dictate my mood, it's nobody's fault but mine. The goal for today: Control my emotions and know that happiness comes when I change how I feel—not how you act! Have a great day, everybody!

Fulfilled

We can do anything that we put our minds to, but we feel truly alive when we do what we set our hearts on. The goal for today: Be passionate about Life. Love people. Help people. Be a part of Life. Do what's Right. Pull my weight. Enjoy every moment, good, bad or otherwise. Breathe Life in. Love the things we want to do and the things we have to do, and at the end of this glorious day, rest our heads on our pillows, not because we're exhausted, but because we feel fulfilled! Have a great day, everybody!

I Don't Know

I went to a friend and told him all my problems and every time he suggested a solution, my response would be "I know!" After about half an hour, he finally said, "Well if you know, why don't you start doing it?" The fact of the matter was that I *didn't* know or I wouldn't have been there asking him what to do. So I was either afraid to admit that I didn't know, or afraid to do what I knew I needed to do. Either way *fear* was the problem and there is only one solution to fear—courage. The goal for today: If I don't know, find out; if I do know ... do it! Have a great day, everybody!

Fill the Void

If I want peace and contentment—trust and security—Life and Love, then I need to learn where these things really come from. I spent years looking outside of myself for these things and I know how cliché it sounds, but it's true: They really do come from inside. For years I felt this void and it was because I thought peace came from my surroundings. I thought trust came from people telling me the truth. I thought Love was something I "got" from someone. The goal for today: Find peace, security and Love within. And fill the void! Have a great day, everybody!

MARCH 13

Be the Solution

"You are the solution!"

This is another one of those "good news-bad news" statements. It holds me accountable for my own life and actions, but at the same time, it fills me full of hope to know that there is a solution, and it's not outside of my control. I spent years waiting for someone else to fix my problems and nothing happened, but the instant that I took the responsibility on myself, things started to change for the better. The goal for today: Don't blame others for the problem or wait for others to fix it ... be the solution! Have a great day, everybody!

March 14

Truth, Faith, and Love

In the absence of fear there can be only Love and in the presence of Love there can be only good. If I have a problem today, it's because I have a fear and the key to getting rid of fear is awareness, understanding and Love. Self-analysis is a dying art, but if I really want to be happy, I need to look at myself. I need to admit that me and my fear caused the problem ... know that faith and self-esteem will solve it ... and then I'm free to Love, which will make my life and yours better. The goal for today: Truth, Faith and Love! Have a great day, everybody!

Could It Be That Simple?

Our minds build our lives, and what we allow to take place there will determine what kind of world we live in. If I spend my time thinking about pain, suffering and misery, then that's what my life will become. If I spend my time thinking about peace, Love and happiness, then that's what my life will become. It doesn't seem like it could be that simple—but it is! The goal for today: Think Right and watch my mind build one beautiful day! Have a great day, everybody!

MARCH 16

Start Living Like It

If there is a God, would He want me to shoot up a school yard? If there is a God, would He want me to cheat on my spouse? If there is a God, would He want me to sign an 1800 page bill without reading it first? If there is a God, would He want me to live in a continual state of war? If there is a God, would He want me to slander people? If there is a God, I am absolutely certain that He would want me to Love you! The goal for today: Whether I believe in God or not, I should start living like it! Have a great day, everybody!

If I'm Thinking Right

I actually can't have a bad day if I'm thinking Right. If I'm thinking Right, I won't overlook the beauty in the world today. If I'm thinking Right, I will view obstacles as opportunities. If I'm thinking Right, I won't allow the words or deeds of others to negatively affect me. If I'm thinking Right, I won't be causing problems in other people's lives today. If I'm thinking Right, I can take a positive approach to ANY and ALL situations that take place in my life today. The goal for today: Think Right! Have a great day, everybody!

March 18

Attention

We need to look for positives. We need to stop giving so much of our time and attention to negatives. If I can't acknowledge at least one good thing in my life today, it's because I'm not looking. It's NEVER because nothing good happened—it's ALWAYS because I failed to see it. Good is taking place all around us ... all day ... every day. Let's not miss it because we are too busy with our problems. The goal for today: Know that if I give more attention to good than bad, my life will get better! Have a great day, everybody!

MARCH 19

Rise Above

I found a way of life, which at first, sounded like it was asking me to be a doormat. I have since come to realize that it was not asking me to roll over—it was asking me to rise above. Rising above is a flawless strategy for happiness. It is my duty to be kind to people and not try to hurt them. The other half of this sacred duty is to not allow myself to be hurt by others. It's a high standard. I try not to hurt or be hurt. Obviously, I don't practice this perfectly, but I'm sure as hell going to try today! Have a great day, everybody!

MARCH 20

⌐

A Better Way

"We always have the choice of learning through spiritual unfoldment, or painful experience and it's our own fault if we choose the latter." —Emmet Fox

I think the lesson that I'm supposed to learn through all of my pain and suffering is that I don't have to experience pain and suffering to learn. As soon as I stop accepting pain and suffering as a "necessary" part of life, then that pain and suffering will end. The goal for today: Stop celebrating my pain and suffering, and start learning a better way! Have a great day, everybody!

MARCH 21

⇥

Spirit

We have written many laws, but we still have crime .... Why? Because the letter of the law says "Don't murder," but the spirit of the law says "Love" and we ignore the spirit. We have written many prayers, but we still have sin.... Why? Because the letter of the prayer says "Thy will be done," but the spirit says "Sincerity gives prayer power." I can't just say it—I have to mean it! If we really want to fix our problems, we must understand, practice and teach this spirit, until every man, woman and child in this world gets it. Have a spiritual day, everybody!

Then You Know

A friend suggested that I frequently ask God to direct my thinking. If you don't believe in God, then ask "If there is a God ... I ask that You direct my thinking." Keep asking until the voice in your head says "Help others" and when you hear that, you know it's God and you should do what He says. I tried it, and sure enough it worked. And it didn't just work once, it works every time that I honestly and genuinely do it. The goal for today: Avoid feeling lonely, angry or depressed by asking God to help me, be helpful to others! Have a great day, everybody!

MARCH 23

Be Powerful

I once was powerless over people, places and things. What does that mean? I'm powerless if I let people dictate my mood ... if I let my environment dictate who I am ... if I let material things dictate my worth. How do I correct this problem? I choose to be happy, regardless of what anyone says or does. I choose to be defined by where my heart is, not where my house is. I choose to base my worth on peace, Love and altruism—not money, cars and houses. The goal for today: Be powerful! Have a great day, everybody!

March 24

Forgiving

Forgiveness is an inside job and it doesn't matter if we are talking about giving it or getting it. I can forgive myself whether you forgive me or not, but part of forgiving myself will depend upon my willingness to forgive others. If I'm doing the best I can today, God will forgive me. If I'm doing the best I can today, I will forgive me. If I'm doing the best I can today, I will forgive you! The goal for today: Remember that "It is by forgiving that one is forgiven" —St. Francis of Assisi. Have a great day, everybody!

MARCH 25

The Good Is Everyone

There is good in everyone. There is not a human being on earth that is incapable of good. When we do bad, it's not because we are bad people, it's because we fearfully believed a lie. I thought revenge would make me feel good. I thought not telling the truth would prevent a problem. I thought putting me first would make my life better ... and I did this all based on fear. The goal for today: Know that Love always feels better. Truth always heals. Selflessness always fulfills and Knowing ends fear! Have a great day, everybody!

Peace Simplified

"In His Will is our peace." —Dante

Simplifying my life has enriched my life. If I'm not at peace, it's because I'm doing something wrong. If I am at peace, it's because I'm doing something Right. It is that simple! When I say simple, I don't mean ignorant. I'm not suggesting that we shouldn't learn and grow and build—I'm suggesting that it shouldn't take me years to explain to you where peace comes from. The goal for today: Know that peace comes from doing the Right thing for the Right reason! Have a great day, everybody!

MARCH 27

A Seeming Contradiction

A paradox is when something seems like a contradiction, but it really isn't. Example: The only way to help myself is to help others. I often hear it said that "I have to do what's best for me" and I agree, but I must understand that "what's best for me" is to help you. The logic behind this paradox is that when I have a problem, helping others clears my mind, making it easier to solve my own problem. If I've got a problem today, I'm going to find someone to help—I just might tell them exactly what I need to hear. Have a great day, everybody!

Take Your Own Advice

If I have a problem, I should ask myself what I would tell other people if they were having the same problem. Putting myself in someone else's shoes is a great way to solve my own problems. Example: If someone is feeling depressed, I would suggest that he or she find someone to be kind and helpful to. So if I'm depressed, what should I do? You guessed it— find someone to be kind and helpful to. The goal for today: Give sound, fact-based advice and then proceed to follow it myself! Have a great day, everybody!

March 29

Gain Immensely

There were things that I refused to believe, because believing them would involve admitting I was wrong. It wasn't until I became willing to admit that I was wrong, that I began to really see the Truth. With an open mind, I can see the Truth about me, the Truth about you, and the Truth about the world around us. I can solve problems ... help you solve problems and maybe even avoid some problems. The goal for today: Open my mind ... practice humility and gain immensely in Peace and Freedom! Have a great day, everybody!

MARCH 30

A Good Life

There are four parts to human nature: physical, emotional, mental and spiritual. Every day (usually without realizing it) we choose which one will govern our lives. Most of my life I was on an emotional roller coaster. My brain wouldn't let me sleep or even function normally and when I overvalued material things, the wheels really came off. Today, I'm going to try it in this order: if I let God (spiritual) direct my thinking (mental), I will feel right (emotional) and the end result will be a good life (physical). Have a great day, everybody!

Rethink It

"The beginning of all expression is thought."
—Emmet Fox

Profoundly important! Nothing ever happened until after it happened in someone's mind first. I can't get up out of my chair until my brain tells my legs to do so. What makes this tricky is that some thoughts are subconscious and therefore we are unaware of them, nevertheless ... the thought did take place. The goal for today: If something isn't going right, I should stop, take a deep breath and rethink it—because the Right thought will always lead to the Right outcome! Have a great day, everybody!

APRIL 1

Win, Lose, or Draw

I am of the strong belief that it is just as important to learn how to lose graciously as it is to win humbly. Shielding ourselves and our children from loss is robbing us all of the opportunity to build character. As a young person, I won a lot and I learned how to do it without getting cocky. Later in life, as I began to experience loss, I was ill-equipped to handle it and I suffered as a result ... but finally learned how to lose and not go off the deep end. The goal for today: Build character through mental stability and balanced emotions— win, lose or draw! Have a great day, everybody!

April 2

My Choice

Before I run around "speaking the truth" or "telling it like it is," I should learn how to find out what the Truth is. If I'm going to tell somebody how I really feel, I should know how I really feel and the fact of the matter is, that it is NEVER someone else's fault that I feel the way I feel. Negative feelings are always, without exception, caused by fear ... they are never caused by your actions! The goal for today: Be responsible for my own feelings, for after all, they are ALWAYS my choice! Have a great day, everybody!

April 3

My Way ... or the Right Way

Talking to a friend I said, "Telling the Truth will insure that the Right thing happens." I followed it up by saying that it might not turn out the way you want, but it will be the Right way. I'm glad I said it and got the point across, but it's been bothering me ever since. Why in the world would I want something to turn out my way instead of the Right way? When did I become convinced that my way would be better than the Right way? The goal for today: Want the Right way and my way to be the same! Have a great day, everybody!

Servant or Ally?

There is an ancient order of monks called the Celi De or Culdee. They are an intriguing group. There are many interesting stories that swirl around them. I enjoy these stories, but what really interests me here is that the name "Celi De" has two interpretations that may sound similar ... but they are very, very different.

1) Sworn servant to God.

2) Sworn ally to God.

The goal for today: Know that God doesn't want me to grovel before Him. He wants me to rise up and stand beside Him! Have a great

Give You His Love

I don't think God wants me to give Him "my" love... I think He wants me to give you His Love. In my mind, Love works like electricity. It flows from the main, through the switch, out to the bulb. God is the main. His Love flows into us and we serve as the switch and if we flick the switch to on, then God's Light or Love can pass through us and shine brightly out into the world. Loving God while hating my neighbor is not the way that this was designed to work. The goal for today: Give you His Love! Have a great day, everybody!

Why Are We Here?

It took me awhile, but today I know who I am. I know what I'm worth. I know why I'm here. I am a human being, spiritual in nature, of infinite value ... here to learn and teach Love... and so are you! Contrary to popular belief, we're all created equal. That doesn't mean that we will all have the same amount of money or the same size house. It means that we are all sent here with the same set of spiritual tools to carry out the same set of spiritual principles. The goal for today: Prove my worth by doing what I was sent here to do—Love! Have a great day, everybody!

APRIL 7

Principle-Based Common Sense

I like dealing with Principles because they apply to all aspects of our lives. Example: I recently said that I should take my own advice and Principle says that if I don't, things will go wrong. Personally: I shouldn't tell my family to do what I say, not what I do. Nationally: We shouldn't write laws that apply to the people, but not to the lawmakers. Worldly: We shouldn't have the leaders of failing nations telling the rest of the world how to live. The goal for today: Principle-based common sense! Have a great day, everybody!

What I Want to Hear

When I'm struggling with a problem, it's because I'm trying to convince myself of a lie. If I spend hours ... days ... weeks ... racking my brains to find a solution, it's because the simple and obvious Truth, isn't what I want to hear. Of course this takes place subconsciously, because no sane person would pretend to look for a solution when he or she doesn't really want one. The Law of Life says if you WANT the Truth, you'll have it. The goal for today: Remember that I have to want the Truth to know the Truth and I have to know the Truth to be set Free! Have a great day, everybody!

Not Because It Can't Be

My life isn't perfect, but it's not because it can't be. The Principles that govern our lives are absolutely perfect—I simply don't practice them perfectly. I spent years telling myself that my problems were unsolvable, that you didn't understand, that happiness was a lost cause, but I was wrong! The goal for today: Know that there is no such thing as an unsolvable problem—that we all have the same problems and that happiness is a very attainable state of mind for any and all of us! Have a great day, everybody!

April 10

Factual Unity Heals

The last thing this world needs is another opinion— everybody has one and most of them are wrong. How can we tell they're wrong? Because if they were right, we could prove them and then we would call them facts. Anything of any real value can be proven and we need to be willing to put the effort into finding the Truth—the facts! Opinions divide us, facts unite us, and without unity we have nothing. The goal for today: Find the facts ... restore unity ... seize the day! Have a great day, everybody!

APRIL 11

~

All the Time

"Those of us who have come to make regular use of prayer would no more do without it than we would refuse air, food, or sunshine."

I pray and I do it frequently because it helps keep me grounded. It brings balance and sanity to my daily life. So when my balance or my thinking is a little off, I don't have to wonder why—it's because I didn't pray. The goal for today: Find something that makes me a better person, a better partner, a better parent, a better friend, a better worker and then do it ... all the time! Have a great day, everybody!

April 12

Confident

I used to be afraid of not having all the answers. I thought I would be viewed as stupid. Once I started finding the answers, then I was afraid of being arrogant. I thought I would be viewed as a know-it-all. I want to be somewhere in between. I don't know everything but I have learned a lot and the most important thing I've learned is that the Truth is always available, if I'm willing to put the effort into finding it. The goal for today: If I don't know, I will admit that and then go find the answers! Have a great day, everybody!

APRIL 13

⌇

Right Feels Good

There is a Principle that says I can't do something good and feel bad about it. If I feel bad about doing something good, it's because some part of what I did was based on fear and selfishness. This same Principle says I can't do something bad and feel good about it. If I feel good about doing something wrong, it's a dishonest, false feeling and it will fall through eventually. The goal for today: Do the Right thing for the Right reason and feel good! Have a great day, everybody!

APRIL 14

Righteous Judgment

If someone makes a mistake I should judge the mistake, not the person. I should acknowledge the mistake—learn from it and then drop it from my thought. It is incredibly unhealthy to dwell on mistakes and to condemn people for making mistakes. If I judge maliciously, then I add to the problem; if I judge the mistake in an attempt to learn and grow and help others, then I'm judging properly. The goal for today: Use the mistakes that we ALL make as an opportunity to learn and grow together! Have a great day, everybody!

APRIL 15

From Within

There are seven things that I spent my whole life looking for outside of myself that can only be found inside: Life - Love - Spirit - Soul - Truth - Intelligence - Principle. I'll do my best to briefly explain a couple of them. The ones that I was most lost about were Love, Truth, and Intelligence.

Intelligence—I was always afraid that I wasn't smart enough because I wasn't very "book smart." Well, now I know that what you get out of books is information, not intelligence. Real intelligence is when I take the information in my head and let my heart tell me whether or not it's accurate. So intelligence comes from inside.

Truth—I had trust issues my whole life because people were always lying to me. I thought I couldn't know the Truth unless someone told me the Truth. Well, now I know that the Truth also comes from within and all I need to do is pay closer attention to actions than words and I'll know the Truth. When I'm relying on my God-given intuition, I can tell when people are lying. I can know the Truth whether you tell me it or not.

Love—An impersonal sense of goodwill toward all. This is the one that the whole world is confused about! We are all born with a heart full of Love and if we give it out freely to others (because it's the right thing to do, not because we are afraid of being alone) it will always be replenished from within. Contrary to popular belief, Love is not something that we get, it is something that we give. One of my favorite quotes is "Love will never look for a quid pro quo" —Emmet Fox. This very simply means that I should never give Love, looking to get it back from that person—it is an inner resource.

The goal for today: Stop looking outside for inner resources!

APRIL 16

~

Don't Get Caught

Motives mean everything! When my life sucked and I asked why, I was told it was because I was selfish. I refused to believe that. I was nice to people, I did things for people, I was loving and caring and giving ... or so I thought. What I failed to realize was that I did it for all the wrong reasons. Loving to get love in return isn't really love. Appearing to care to build my reputation isn't really caring. Giving people what they want so I can get what I want isn't really giving. The goal for today: Do something nice for someone and don't get caught! Have a great day, everybody!

Our Only Aim

"To be helpful is our only aim."

I used to help people so they would tell others what a great guy I was or how smart I was. I might even intentionally help you the wrong way so I could get what I wanted. I didn't do these things to hurt people, I did them because I was afraid. I was afraid that people wouldn't like me ... I was afraid that I wasn't smart enough ... I was terrified that I might end up alone in this life. I've worked hard to get rid of these fears and the goal for today is to help people because it's the Right thing to do! Have a great day, everybody!

Have it All

I once asked someone, "Will things ever turn out the way I want them to?" and she said "Yes—as soon as you want the 'Right' thing." For a long time I *thought* I knew what I wanted and little by little, as I began to get it, I realized it wasn't what I really wanted at all. Now I know exactly who I am and exactly what I want! I want what's fair and just. I want what's best for everybody, not just me, and I want to help others to want the same. The goal for today: Want the Right things and have it all! Have a great day, everybody!

APRIL 19

When Hope Turns Into Action

I used to hope that life would get better ... that things would change ... that happiness would return. It wasn't until that hope turned into action that things began to happen. Hope is a wonderful and necessary part of success, but hope alone isn't enough. Life doesn't get better all by itself. Change doesn't happen without action. Happiness is the direct result of *doing* what I know in my heart is Right. The goal for today: Go beyond hope and take action, because that's when the good stuff starts happening! Have a great day, everybody!

Right Here and Now

"Love each other." —Jesus

The real purpose for our human existence is to learn how to Love each other, and I can't think of a better place and time to start than right here and now! The goal for today: Love everyone I come in contact with, because the only way to truly experience Love is to give it out freely to others! Have a great day, everybody!

April 21

The First Principle

The First Principle: You can't fix a problem that you refuse to admit exists. Example: I've had many failed relationships and in my mind, it was always the other person's fault. In this delusional state, I would end the relationship ... change nothing ... start a new one and repeat the vicious cycle. Once I admitted that I was at least partially responsible and took a look at myself, then I was able to make some changes and correct the problem. The goal for today: Admit my faults, because admission is the beginning of the end of the problem! Have a great day, everybody!

The Second Principle

The Second Principle: You can't solve a problem with the same mind that created it. I know the word "God" makes some people uncomfortable, but hear me out. There is a voice deep down inside of every man, woman and child that whispers the Truth. There are a million other voices screaming in our heads, but that quiet whisper coming from your heart is the voice of reason—the Truth! Sane people don't do what they know in their heart is wrong. The goal for today: Before I turn on my phone, my computer, my TV, I'll listen to my heart because that's where sanity comes from! Have a great day, everybody!

APRIL 23

꘡

The Third Principle

The Third Principle: I can't rely on God and play God at the same time. I said yesterday that God is that whisper of Truth in our hearts and once I begin to hear that whisper, I have a decision to make. All day, every day, I decide whether I'm going to do what I *know* in my heart is Right (God's will)... or do what I *think* in my head is right (my will). The goal for today: Ask myself, "If there is a God... would He want me to do what I'm about to do?" and then actually do it! Have a great day, everybody!

April 24

The Fourth Principle

The Fourth Principle: No defect can be corrected until we clearly see what it is. For years I treated the symptoms of my problems instead of the causes. Example: I thought the solution to my fear of being alone was to not be alone. I was wrong. Did you ever feel alone in a room full of people? Me too! That's because loneliness is just a symptom. *Fear* is the real problem and until I fix that, I will continue to feel alone no matter how many people I surround myself with. The goal for today: Stop treating symptoms ... treat causes! Have a great day, everybody!

The Fifth Principle

The Fifth Principle: There is no real freedom without admitting my faults. Obviously I have to admit my mistakes to myself and to God, but it is equally as important to admit them to another human being. Why? Because I become a slave to my mistakes when I'm afraid to admit them to my peers. Humility breeds humility, whereas a refusal to admit our mistakes creates animosity and discord. Humility is defined as having or showing a consciousness of one's defects; modest ... and that sounds like a good idea today. Have a great day, everybody!

The Sixth Principle

The Sixth Principle: My defects can't be corrected against my will. The key to solving problems is to spot, admit and correct them. We spotted our defects in the Fourth Principle and admitted them in the Fifth. Now we set out to correct them and this Sixth Principle is where correction begins. We are all born with Free Will, but what does that really mean? I think Thomas Jefferson said it best when he said "God Himself will not save men against their wills." The goal for today: Willingness ... because I can't correct my problems without it! Have a great day, everybody!

The Seventh Principle

The Seventh Principle: God will remove my defects, if I ask. Once I'm willing to let go of a problem, all I have to do is ask. There is a catch, however—my appeal to God must be sincere and unselfish. I can't trick God and selfish prayers go unanswered. I shouldn't ask God to remove my problems so I can feel better. I should ask Him to remove my problems so I can be helpful to others. The goal for today: Know that "Ask and ye shall receive" is true so long as I ask for the Right things ... for the Right reasons! Have a great day, everybody!

The Eighth Principle

The Eighth Principle: Amends are impossible without willingness. This is the third time we have mentioned willingness and its vital importance in making any real forward progress. Throughout this process I've come to realize that I've hurt people and it's time to mend these broken human relations. It may require a lot of willingness to go to someone, admit my mistakes and attempt to prove that I've changed, but it must be done in order to fix this. The goal for today: Be willing to take a different approach ... be willing to change! Have a great day, everybody!

The Ninth Principle

The Ninth Principle: I must make amends in order to repair damaged relationships. Now that I'm willing to make amends, it's time to go do it. The first thing to realize is that the word *amend* is different from the word *apologize*. Amend means to change, so I can't just mumble "I'm sorry" under my breath and think that's sufficient. I'm going to prove to you, through my actions, that I'm sorry. I'm going to think and speak and act differently toward you. The goal for today: Change is the only constant … it's time to embrace it rather than fear it! Have a great day, everybody!

APRIL 30

⌐

The Tenth Principle

The Tenth Principle: I must maintain my growth or lose it. This Principle keeps me from taking one step forward and two steps back. Now that I admitted the problem (1); became willing to believe there is a better way and committed to following it (2 and 3); proceeded to spot, admit and correct past mistakes (4 through 9); it's time to live this way on a regular basis. This is my lookout and if I practice it diligently, I will begin to catch my mistakes before they happen. The goal for today: Pay attention! Have a great day, everybody!

May 1

The Eleventh Principle

The 11th Principle: Growth and forward progress are required to be successful at life. First thing in the morning I want to get my mind pointed in the Right direction (I ask God to direct my thinking). The idea is simple: Negative thoughts bring negative results. Positive thoughts bring positive results and I want to start off on a positive. At day's end, I want to take an honest inventory of the day's events. I'll take comfort in things well done and constructively criticize my mistakes. The goal for today: Bookend my day with growth and guides to progress! Have a great day, everybody!

MAY 2

The Twelfth Principle

The Twelfth Principle: Share my happiness or lose it. Throughout this whole process, I've learned a lot about God, about myself and about others. Now it's time to live by what I've learned and pass on what I've learned to anyone else who cares to have it. If I freely, enthusiastically, and willingly carry this message of hope to those who want and need it badly, I am guaranteed happiness. The goal for today: Do what I was put here to do—trust God—clean house—help others! Have a great day, everybody!

May 3

Truth Is Never Bad

The Truth can never be a bad thing! If something bad happens to me as the result of telling the Truth, then it either wasn't the Truth, or what happened wasn't really bad. Example: I thought telling the Truth about my mistakes was going to make me look stupid, ruin my reputation and cause people to not want to be around me. But the exact opposite happened—people viewed it as intelligent, respected me for it and were attracted to my honesty. The goal for today: Know that the real Truth always makes things better! Have a great day, everybody!

MAY 4

What's on Your Mind?

Did you ever get in trouble for speaking your mind? Yeah, me too. I got in trouble because what was on my mind was all the wrong stuff. I thought it was your fault that I was angry, frustrated, sad, lonely and just generally unhappy. The fact of the matter is that my feelings come from inside of me, not outside. I wasn't getting in trouble for speaking my mind, I was getting in trouble because what I was saying wasn't true. The goal for today: Have kind and Loving stuff on my mind and I won't ever have to be afraid to speak it! Have a great day, everybody!

Change Yourslf ... Change the World

I no longer live under the delusion that what is taking place around me dictates who I am. I have come to the absolute conclusion that it's what takes place inside of me that controls my outer circumstances. Our environment doesn't create our personalities, our personalities create our environment. We need to learn for ourselves and then teach our children that our hearts and minds should run our lives, not our surroundings. The goal for today: Know that changing myself is what will ultimately change the world! Have a great day, everybody!

Must I?

If I'm criticized, can I decide how I feel about it or is my only choice feeling hurt? If society does wrong, can I decide what to do or is my only choice doing wrong? If I come from a troubled past, can I decide my future or do I have no choice–except to fail at life? For years I believed that people controlled my feelings ... society forced my actions ... my past dictated my future and yet again ... I was wrong. The goal for today: Rise above this false belief and claim what is Rightfully mine—Happiness, Peace and Freedom! Have a great day, everybody!

Autonomy

Autonomy is defined as self-governing. If we really want to reduce crime, fix our economy and find some real Peace in this world, we must practice autonomy! My Heart is my ruler and my conscience my cabinet. What the hell does that mean? It means that we wouldn't need a billion rules and regulations to tell us what's right and what's wrong if we would simply consult our own conscience and get in the habit of listening to it. The goal for today: Autonomy. If there is a God, would He want me to do what I'm about to do? Have a great day, everybody!

May 8

Not Sad? Or Supremely Happy

I can take a pill that turns off my emotions to avoid feeling sad, but that pill will never, ever, EVER make me happy! I came to a point in my life where just not feeling anxious or depressed was no longer good enough; I wanted to be happy—truly happy! If I strive for real happiness and become willing to do whatever it takes to get it, then I will move in that direction and that's what I intend to do. The goal for today: Don't settle for "not sad." Strive to be supremely happy! Have a great day, everybody!

Through Me, to Help You

"We must not fly in the face of the Law by expecting it to do for us what it can only do through us."
—*Thomas Troward*

Notice that the word *Law* is capitalized. That means Troward is talking about God. God works through us, not for us. And once we fully understand what that means, things begin to make sense. The will of God is ALWAYS good. Bad things happen when I don't allow His will to flow freely through me. The goal for today: Don't expect God to do things *for* me. Let Him work *through* me ... to help you! Have a great day, everybody!

Supposed to Be Happy

At the height of my depression and misery, someone said to me: "You're right where you're supposed to be." I remember thinking, if this miserable state is where I'm supposed to be, then I don't even want to live anymore. Fortunately I hung in there, found some REAL help and got my life turned around. Here is what I learned: I'm supposed to be happy and if I'm not, then I'm not "where I'm supposed to be." The goal for today: Do whatever it takes to be happy ... because that's where I'm supposed to be! Have a great day, everybody!

MAY 11

The Stream of Life

"Were we thinking of ourselves most of the time? Or were we thinking of what we could do for others, of what we could pack into the stream of life?"

I love this quote and I have gone through every emotion with it. At first I *thought* I was thinking of others, but in reality I would only help you if it benefitted me. Then, once I knew the Truth about my selfishness, the question was laughable. I was always thinking about myself. Now, I can honestly say that I have your well-being before mine, more often than not. The goal for today: Have a genuine concern for the well-being of others! Have a great day, everybody!

MAY 12

Be Set Free

Do you have a bad habit that you'd like to give up? I've had many and here is what I learned: There is only one Right way to break a bad habit and that's to get rid of the desire to do it. Nothing else can bring permanent results. Avoiding temptation, keeping really busy, even rehabilitation might work for a little while. But there is only one way to banish a bad habit permanently and that's to have an Honest desire to stop. The goal for today: Don't just avoid temptation ... rid my heart and mind of the desire to do wrong and be set Free! Have a great day, everybody!

MAY 13

Positively Derogatory

I think I created a new catch phrase, "Positively Derogatory." That's when I inspire myself by bashing the hell out of others. Saying rotten things about other people in an attempt to feel better about myself is crazy! I've done it many times in my life and I have come to the conclusion that it's a terrible idea. Now that I've regained some sanity, I've found a better way. The goal for today: Rather than put you down, I should try to lift myself and others up by being the best person I know how to be! Have a great day, everybody!

MAY 14

Handle the Truth

"You can't handle the truth." This statement was very true most of my life. I was scared to death of the Truth ... primarily because knowing it would mean that I should adhere to it. There were some things that, deep down, I knew I shouldn't be doing and other things I knew I should be and until I was ready to make those changes. I couldn't handle the Truth. Now that I am willing to change and embrace the Truth, I no longer have to live in fear of it. The goal for today: Handle the Truth! Have a great day, everybody!

May 15

Faith ... Not Fear

"Faith (not blind belief, but understanding faith) may be thought of as wisdom in action."
—*Emmet Fox*

When I know, in my head and in my heart, what the Right thing to do is, I can take that action without fear because the Right action can only lead to the Right outcome. Real faith isn't about differentiating Right from wrong, it's about believing that the Right outcome is the one I really want. The goal for today: Get my head and my heart on the same page and act on faith, not fear! Have a great day, everybody!

MAY 16

Subtle Selfishness

Someone once said to me, "Your son wants and needs for you to be happy. Are you willing to go to any length to achieve that goal for his sake?" Of course my answer was yes, but my actions proved otherwise. I now realize that I had a subtle form of selfishness that couldn't be corrected without help. I didn't intend to hurt my son, but the selfishness, that contributed to my unhappiness caused me to do just that. The goal for today: Do whatever it takes to spot, admit and correct this subtle selfishness, for everyone's sake! Have a great day, everybody!

May 17

Anger Is Really Fear

People are never mean just because they like to be mean. People are always mean because they are afraid of something. Notice that I used the words "never" and "always." These words are absolutes and I don't throw them around lightly. It is humanly impossible to be angry without first being afraid. The goal for today: I will fully acknowledge and understand that anger is really fear. If it crops up in me, I will spot, admit and correct it. If it crops up in you, I will treat it accordingly, with patience, tolerance, kindliness and love! Have a great day, everybody!

MAY 18

Succeed at Life

The value of understanding the Principles that govern our lives is immeasurable. A Principle, by definition, is infallible and once I fully understand that, I will stop trying to find ways around these Laws of Life. Gravity is a Principle and no one questions it. But when I say "I can't be selfish and happy" is a Principle, everyone questions it. It doesn't matter what your definition of selfishness or happiness is, the fact remains—it can't be done. The goal for today: Work with the Principles, instead of against them ... and succeed at Life! Have a great day, everybody!

May 19

Follow the Plan

God is the architect and His blueprint is Perfect. Flawless. We are the builders and it is our job to carry out this perfect plan to the best of our ability. Now that I fully understand that, I can stop blaming God for the troubles of this world. It is I that misinterpreted the floor plan. We hate, when the plan said to Love; we take, when the plan said to Give; we fear, when the plan calls for Faith and we lie, when the plan calls for the Truth. The goal for today: Follow the plan! Have a great day, everybody!

MAY 20

Give Everything

I once thought, "I give too much. I care too much. I'm too kind." When giving, caring and kindness turn into a bad thing, it's because I'm doing it out of fear rather than doing it the Right way ... for the Right reasons. I tarnish these things when I'm afraid of what others think of me ... when I'm afraid of being alone ... when I'm afraid of confrontation. When I'm doing these things for the Right reasons, I can never do them too much. The goal for today: Get rid of fear and give everything, care with my whole heart, and be kind to everyone! Have a great day, everybody!

MAY 21

A Positive Foundation

The fear of being alone has caused me to do all sorts of crazy things and one of them was to seek attention through self-pity. Self-pity is not a very attractive quality and now I can see that I should never want people to hang out with me because they feel sorry for me. That kind of companionship never lasts because it is built on a negative foundation. If I want real, happy, healthy, lasting companionship it must be built on a positive foundation. The goal for today: Attract people to me by giving Honesty, Purity, Selflessness and Love! Have a great day, everybody!

MAY 22

No Matter What!

Fixing a broken human relationship is how we further our common humanity and is the most important undertaking that any of us will ever embark upon! When we refuse to Love each other, no matter what good reason we think we have, we destroy our purpose for existing. We are all in this together. We need to Love each other. We need to be Honest with each other. We need to give to each other and we need to do it simply because it's the Right thing to do for each other. The goal for today: Love each other ... no matter what! Have a great day, everybody!

MAY 23

Help You Help Yourself

I asked a friend for advice and he said "Did you ask God first?" Of course I hadn't but I didn't want to say that so I said "Well, God works through people. I'm asking you." I can see now that I was scared and lazy. I didn't want to do the work and I was afraid I wouldn't get the Right answers. Now I see things differently. I do believe that God works through people, but I also believe that my job, when trying to help people, is to refer them back to God—He knows best. The goal for today: Help you help yourself! Have a great day, everybody!

May 24

Honestly Want

I can't force myself to do what's Right on any lasting or permanent basis. Eventually I will have to HONESTLY WANT to do what's Right, or slip back into my old ways. And I have come to the realization that in order to honestly want to do what's Right, I must know that the outcome will be good. Doing something just because you know you should doesn't feel nearly as good as doing it because you really want to. The goal for today: Get excited about doing what's Right, knowing that nothing feels better! Have a great day, everybody!

MAY 25

Follow Your Heart to Freedom

Our founding fathers were commonly referred to as "Free Thinkers." What does that mean? They thought for themselves and encouraged others to do the same. They were not being blindly led by anyone, not by the church nor the political world. They were being led by their hearts and minds ... their instincts and intuition ... by their God-consciousness. Blindly following is not Freedom. Freedom is doing what we know in our heart is Right, not what someone else tells us is right. The goal for today: Know that God gave us brains to use! Have a great day, everybody!

Sacrifice

"Ask not what your country can do for you, ask what you can do for your country." —John F. Kennedy

There is no greater sacrifice for your country, than to lay down your life in defense of it! The American flag is a symbol of Peace and Freedom ... Liberty and Justice ... Faith and Courage ... and that is what the bravest of the brave put their lives on the line for. They don't risk all for government or politics, they risk all for the Love of God and country, for family, and for each other. The goal for today: Honor their courage, their devotion, and their sacrifice. Live up to the Freedom they fought and died to earn for all of us! Happy Memorial Day! Have a great day, everybody!

Fearlessly Honest

"We must be entirely honest with somebody if we expect to live long or happily in this world."

I've made many mistakes in life and the less willing I was to admit them, the more I found myself repeating them. Honesty should never be scary. It is a healing and redeeming quality that can only bring about good when properly carried out. Lies never fix a problem, they hide the problem or make it worse. The goal for today: Be fearlessly honest about myself, because it solves problems and encourages others to do the same! Have a great day, everybody!

MAY 28

A Good Liar

"It takes one to know one."

I have been taught how to see through my own lies and as a result, I can see through yours too. It's easy to lie to doctors and psychiatrists ... to family and friends ... even to ourselves ... but it's nearly impossible to lie to a good liar. My past was once a terrible liability, but now it is a valuable asset. Now I can help people because of it. The goal for today: If you need to know the Truth, ask a reformed liar ... for there is no better BS detector! Have a great day, everybody!

MAY 29

Inner Peace Leads to World Peace

Inner Peace ... Domestic Tranquility ... World Peace ... in that order. This is a point of paramount importance! Inner Peace is established by having a genuine concern for the welfare of others. Then large groups of people, unified by Inner Peace, can begin to experience Domestic Tranquility. Then these large groups (nations), unified by Domestic Tranquility, can begin to experience World Peace. This is a scientific equation—it simply cannot work any other way. The goal for today: Inner Peace ... because I can't give what I don't have! Have a great day, everybody!

MAY 30

A Real Difference

Can you tell the difference between the unwilling and the unable? This is important! I Love helping people but it's wrong to give to the unwilling. Emmet Fox says that 'Wisdom is the perfect blending of Intelligence and Love.' If I blindly give because I want to help, intelligence is absent. If I refuse to give for the sake of the bottom line, Love is absent. But if I use my heart and mind, then I can truly help people. The goal for today: Learn how to give to the right people, in the right way, at the right time and make a real difference! Have a great day, everybody!

Humility Breeds Humility

Humility is about admitting my own mistakes. Did you ever point out someone else's mistakes and end up in an argument? Yeah, me too. Did you ever point out your own mistakes to someone else and end up in an argument? Yeah, me neither. This should tell me something. Maybe I should stick to my own mistakes. The goal for today: Know that the best way to point out someone else's mistakes is to point out my own ... because humility breeds humility! Have a great day, everybody!

Learn a Truth

Someone asked me, "Do you think you're honest?" Of course I answered "Yes." Then he started asking questions that proved I had lost touch with the Truth. I claimed to be honest... but blamed others for my feelings. I claimed to be honest... but justified my anger. I claimed to be honest... but lied to myself about many things. Honesty is more than not lying—it's seeking, finding and sharing the real Truth. If I don't tell a lie today, that's great, but if I don't learn a Truth today, then I'm not really practicing Honesty. Have a great day, everybody!

Life Will Get Better If ....

"Putting out of our minds the wrongs others had done, we resolutely looked for our own mistakes."

This is literally a way of life today! Every time I experience negative feelings (depressed, angry, sad, anxious... etc.) I immediately look at myself and my own thoughts and actions. I no longer allow others to dictate my feelings, nor do I blame them for my feelings. The goal for today: Know that my life will not get better by pointing out your mistakes ... but it will if I spot, admit and correct my own! Have a great day, everybody!

Enjoy Peace of Mind

My attitude from moment to moment is what dictates my peace of mind or lack thereof. Example: Sometimes when my cat wakes me up, I get upset ... sometimes I don't. The fact that the same act sometimes bothers me and sometimes doesn't is proof that it has nothing to do with the act—it has everything to do with me. It's amazing how much control we have over our own lives when we realize it. The goal for today: Pay attention, maintain a positive attitude, and enjoy peace of mind! Have a great day, everybody!

Learn How to Think

If people forget my name, what is my first thought? Do I assume that I'm not important or interesting enough to remember? Or that they were a little too busy or nervous and not really paying attention? This is an important question! The first answer shows a lack of self-esteem, which is probably causing all sorts of other problems and we don't even realize it. The second one shows understanding and a sense of rational, realistic thinking that I should be teaching to others. The goal for today: Learn how to think! Have a great day, everybody!

Even When It's for Their Own Good

I never push people to see the Truth about themselves unless they are asking. When I attempt to force the unwilling to see the Truth (even when it's for their own good), it never goes over well. Why are we so hell-bent on telling people the truth about them anyway? The best way to transmit the Truth to people that need it, is to find the Truth about myself and then live in accordance with that Truth. Actions speak louder than words. The goal for today: Don't tell people their truth ... demonstrate the Truth! Have a great day, everybody!

June 6

Natural Life

I am not of the belief that fear, anger and sadness are normal and natural. Just because everybody's doing it, doesn't mean that it's normal and natural—that just means that it has become commonplace. I am of the belief that Happiness, Peace and Freedom are normal and natural. I spent so much time trying to justify my fear, anger and depression that I was missing out on all the joy this life has to offer. The goal for today: Help others and live a truly natural life ... which consists of Happiness, Peace and Freedom! Have a great day, everybody!

Find It and Apply It

I recently saw an episode of *Cops* and an officer said,"Why did you start using drugs again?" and the detainee said, "I wish I knew." This is just one of many examples illustrating the hopeless state of not knowing what makes me tick. If I don't know what caused my problem, then I can't fix it. People don't just wakes up and decide to act like an ass ... they don't know why they do it and neither do the people asking them. The goal for today: Know that there is an answer to our problems. Find it and apply it! Have a great day, everybody

June 8

Construct a Better Life

I had to learn how to constructively criticize myself. I spent far too long swinging from one extreme to the other. I would either refuse to admit that I made a mistake, or become over-remorseful and beat myself up to no end. The happy medium is constructive criticism, which means I can spot, admit and correct mistakes ... rather than hide, fear and ignore them. Today, if I make a mistake, I will admit it, ask God's forgiveness, and put an honest effort into correcting it. Today, I will construct a better life! Have a great day, everybody!

Do What We Do

"If you want what we've got, then do what we do."

A very simple statement that borders on genius! I used to get mad at happy people because they had something I didn't have and it seemed so unfair, but now I can see the Truth. I wasn't unhappy because I got a raw deal, it was because I wasn't doing what they were doing. When we realize that this same Principle applies on the city, state, national and even worldwide levels, this becomes profoundly important! The goal for today: Do what Happy people do! Have a great day, everybody!

June 10

What Do You Believe?

"Choose your own conception of God."

A friend asked me, "Who chose your conception of God for you?" After a prolonged pause, I said "I did." He then said that my idea of God had probably been instilled in me by someone else. That makes perfect sense to me now. It felt so uncomfortable because it wasn't what I believed, it was what someone else told me to believe. The goal for today: Start asking myself, "What do I believe about God?" and rebuild my belief system from the inside out! Have a great day, everybody!

Live It

*"The only knowledge you have is what you practice.
What you read in books you do not have."*
—Emmet Fox

I can't just know how to live a good life, I have
to live a good life. There are a few things that I
know I should be doing differently in my daily
life, but obviously, nothing is going to change
until I actually do something. I must remember that my life will get better when I start doing what I know I need to do to make it better.
The goal for today: Don't just read about life—
live it! Have a great day, everybody!

Spiritual Principles Can

Man-made laws can't fix this, but Spiritual Principles can. To eliminate violence, we must teach that Love is a more powerful ally than hate. To eliminate economic problems, we must teach that giving brings more prosperity than getting. To eliminate deceit, we must teach that the Truth always heals. To eliminate poor decision making, we must teach that faith is a better motive than fear. The goal for today: Know that Purity, Honesty, Selflessness and Love lead to Happiness, Peace and Freedom! Have a great day, everybody!

JUNE 13

For All of Us

There is a fine line between greed and ambition ... between complacency and true contentment. Forward progress is an extremely important part of life, but it means something different to me now. I'm no longer obsessing about material gains—I am trying to move forward in the Right direction. Today I want to make progress in the areas of Peace and Contentment ... Happiness and Harmony ... Freedom and above all Love. And I don't just want these things for me, I want them for all of us! Have a great day, everybody!

Humble, Not Feeble

"He was humble, but willing to fight." —Scott Stapp

He's not angry, he's not arrogant, he's not looking for a fight ... but he's also not going to roll over, he's not a doormat. This is a valuable lesson: Humble and feeble are two different things. I don't believe that we have a God-given right to violent aggression, but I am certain that we do have a God given right to self-defense. The goal for today: Be kind but not weak. Be open but not vulnerable. Bend but don't break! Have a great day, everybody!

Supreme Happiness

Beatitude—a state of supreme happiness. There is an eight-verse prose poem in the Bible called The Beatitudes. It's not just a beautiful poem ... it's a guide to achieving supreme happiness.

1) Get rid of self-will
2) Celebrate the rebirth of God's will
3) Open my mind
4) Vigorously seek the Truth
5) Forgive others
6) Act on faith, not fear
7) Find peace, then spread peace
8) Don't turn a blind eye to my mistakes.

This will lead to Supreme Happiness—Heaven on earth! Have a great day, everybody!

Unable, or Unwilling?

There are those who are willing and able to take care of themselves and they are doing just fine. I should help them help others. There are those who are willing but unable to take care of themselves. I should happily do everything within my means to help them. There are those who are perfectly able but unwilling to take care of themselves. The best way to help them is to teach them to want to take care of themselves. The goal for today: Help the right people, the right way, for the right reason! Have a great day, everybody!

JUNE 17

Unity

"We have a common peril."

Why do marital problems exist ... money problems exist ... drug and alcohol problems exist? Because of selfishness, resentment, dishonesty and fear.

"We have a common solution."

If the cause is selfishness, resentment, dishonesty and fear, there is only one possible solution: Learn how to be Selfless, Loving, Honest and Pure.

"Our common journey."

Those who have solved their problems in this manner should band together to help others do the same. The goal for today: Unity! Have a great day, everybody!

JUNE 18

Damage Control

My old way of life was based on doing whatever the hell I wanted and dealing with the consequences later. Then I found a better way. I learned how to spot, admit and correct my mistakes. And the more I practice this better way, the closer I get to spotting a mistake before it happens, which can keep me from making the mistake to begin with. The goal for today: Think BEFORE I speak or act and stop living in a constant state of damage control! Have a great day, everybody!

Be Free of Anger

"If we were to live, we had to be free of anger."

Wow ... that's asking a lot! How do we begin to achieve this goal? When I catch myself feeling angry or hurt, I try to immediately focus on why I feel that way. I focus on my feelings, not the other person's actions. I can't get angry if I don't think about the other person. I must remember that my feelings don't come from other people's actions—they come from inside of me. The goal for today: Focus on my feelings, rather than your actions ... and be free of anger! Have a great day, everybody!

Actually Care

"This country will not be a good place for any of us to live in unless we make it a good place for all of us to live in." —Theodore Roosevelt

The only way to fix the problems we face in this country and in this world, is to give up our selfish, self-centered ways and actually start caring about each other again—There is no other way! I don't care how many laws we write, or bills we pass. If we don't stop living selfishly, we can't fix this. The goal for today: Actually care about somebody other than myself! Have a great day, everybody!

Listen

We need to learn how to listen. Attention is one of those invaluable assets of life! A friend was telling me a tragic story from her past and after a few brief statements, the trouble became clear and thirty years of pain were corrected in an hour. She told me what the real problem was and she didn't even realize it. Find a trustworthy friend. Tell him or her your story and pay close attention because the Truth is already in your story—you just over-looked it. The goal for today: Listen ... to myself and everybody else, because it just might save a life! Have a great day, everybody!

Pay Attention

"Attention is the key." —Emmet Fox

If I pay attention, I can avoid misery and depression. I can learn the Truth about myself and others. I can cause fewer mistakes and accidents. I can wipe out loneliness, trust issues and self-esteem problems. I can uncover the cause and the solution to all of my problems. We should all find a method of improving our focus and attention (I ask God for help), because it is the key to Life and Happiness for us all. The goal for today: Pay attention! Have a great day, everybody!

Happiness for All

I had a different message prepared for today but a conversation with a friend brought this thought to mind very strongly. I can honestly say that I have no ill will toward anyone today. There is not a person on this planet that I would want something bad to happen to. I'm not feeling angry ... I'm not feeling jealous ... I'm not feeling entitled and I've got to tell you ... it feels pretty damn good! The goal for today: Honestly wish for every human being to experience Happiness, Peace and Freedom! Have a great day, everybody!

Understand and Love

"It's impossible to truly understand someone and not love them." —From the movie Ender's Game

Love is when I have no ill toward people and if I do have ill will toward them, it's because I don't understand them. If people are acting poorly, it is because they are hurt or wounded and in need of help. Sometimes we can help them overcome their problems, but other times we can only help by understanding why they are acting that way and not getting upset. The goal for today: Understand and Love! Have a great day, everybody!

JUNE 25

Admit My Mistakes

There is nothing wrong with being wrong ... but there is something wrong with not admitting when I'm wrong. For some strange reason, I used to believe that it was better to pretend that I didn't ever make a mistake, than to admit it and try to make it right. Everybody makes mistakes and everybody knows that, so who did I think I was fooling? The goal for today: Earn people's trust and respect by admitting my mistakes! Have a great day, everybody!

Know

"I know." —Emmet Fox

I encourage people to think. When people say "I don't know why I did that" or "I don't know why they would do that"... I usually ask them to think about it. Nobody ever does or says anything for no reason and if I take the time to understand the reason, then that particular person or thing can't hurt me anymore. In fact, if I truly understand people, then I can learn and grow and progress as a result of the thing that previously seemed so negative. The goal for today: Know! Have a great day, everybody!

Always a Positive

A friend of mine has recently proven that every cloud literally has a silver lining. If we are willing to look for it, there is an upside to everything. Example: Someone called her fat. She got mad and then realized that the reason she got mad was because she isn't happy about her weight. She started walking and lost ten lbs in a week. When we discussed it, she laughed and said, "Instead of getting mad, I should thank him." The goal for today: Make all things positive! Have a great day, everybody!

June 28

Take the Power Back

I used to be powerless over people, places and things. I allowed people to dictate my feelings and my sense of worth. I allowed my surroundings to dictate my activities, and I allowed *things* to become far too important to me. But not anymore! Now I get to choose how I feel and I know what I'm worth. Now I can make sane, logical decisions about the activities that I partake in from day to day, and I have gotten much better at attaching the appropriate value to material things. The goal for today: Regain control of my own life and feelings! Have a great day, everybody!

Peace and Happiness

For years I couldn't figure out why nothing ever seemed to go my way. Well, I finally figured it out. My way said that my happiness was all that mattered ... that all of my anger was justified ... that concealing the truth was the best way to get what I wanted ... that fear would keep me safe. Technically, I did get my way and it led me to misery and depression. The goal for today: Care about others. Get rid of anger. Tell the Truth. Live Free ... and then I can experience Peace and Happiness! Have a great day, everybody!

Personal Inventory

"... a personal inventory, which many of us had never attempted"

I was told I was selfish and I said "No, I'm not—I'd give you the shirt off my back." I was told I was resentful and I said "No, I'm not— I get along with everybody." I was told I was dishonest and I said "No, I'm not—I always tell the truth." I was told I was afraid and I said "No, I'm not—I'm not afraid of anything." Then I was taught how to take a personal inventory and sure enough, I had all of these defects of character. The goal for today: Keep tabs on myself, because it makes my life and yours better! Have a great day, everybody!

July 1

What People Really Need

In a room full of people a young man needed help. One person offered money, another a ride.... But there was one person there who didn't have anything material to give him, but still offered help. What that person offered was kindness, compassion and a helping hand. So the one person that appeared to have nothing to offer, was the only one offering what this young man really needed—a friend. The goal for today: Give my time ... my love ... my humanity ... because that's what people really need! Have a great day, everybody!

JULY 2

Know It and Share It

Someone asked me why his life was unhappy. I knew the answer, but I was afraid to say it because I didn't want to hurt his feelings. I told him I knew and asked if he was SURE he wanted to know. He said yes, so I proceeded to tell him that his troubles came from being selfish, resentful, dishonest and afraid. As I explained each one in detail, his eyes lit up. He didn't get angry or defensive or hurt—he was happy to finally know the Truth. The goal for today: Know the Truth and share it with anyone who asks! Have a great day, everybody!

Strive for Perfection ... Claim Progress

Being perfect is not important, but *trying* to be perfect is absolutely essential to forward progress. If I'm not trying to be perfect, then I am selling myself short. I'm depriving myself and others of a better life. We are all supposed to be striving for perfection, and falling short simply shows us what we need to work on. I don't beat myself up when I fall short—I simply use it as a guide to progress. The goal for today: Claim progress while striving for perfection! Have a great day, everybody!

July 4

Not Dependent

The word "Independence" means "not dependent." There is no better feeling than the Freedom that comes from taking care of myself. It is incredibly unhealthy to be overly dependent upon anyone or anything. I don't want or need anyone to run my life for me. What I do need is the Love that God fills our hearts with ... and I need to share that Love with you. The goal for today: Remember what independence really means, earn it, and celebrate the brave souls that stood their ground in the name of Liberty and Justice for all! Happy Fourth of July! Have a great day, everybody!

Learn the Science of Life

There is a science to life. There is a distinct reason for every success and every failure. This science says that selflessness can NEVER bring about anger and resentment. A positive can't cause a negative. Example: If I'm mad at someone and claiming that it's because I just want him to be happy, I'm lying to myself. If I get mad, it's because I'm afraid he is going to negatively affect my life. Resentment can ONLY come from selfishness. The goal for today: Learn the science of life and find Freedom! Have a great day, everybody!

Stop Being a Victim

"If you act like prey, you become prey."

My lack of self-esteem put me in a position to be harmed. My fear of making decisions put me in a position to be controlled. My unwillingness to think for myself put me in a position to be misled. My inability to stand on my own two feet put me in a position to be taken advantage of. Now I am willing to do whatever it takes to regain my self-worth, overcome my fears and learn how to think for and take care of myself. The goal for today: Stop being a victim! Have a great day, everybody!

Don't Steal Peace

Who should put more effort into making my life worthwhile: me or you? I had to learn the hard way that Peace and Happiness are an inside job. No one can do it for me. I could be taught, pointed in the right direction, led to water—but when I expect you to work harder for my Happiness than I am willing to work for it, then I haven't earned it, I don't deserve it and I will lose it. Any Peace that I steal from you won't last. I must find my own. The goal for today: Earn what I get out of life! Have a great day, everybody!

Inner Peace Creates Outer Peace

When I wake up, I try to establish some sense of Peace (I choose to pray). If I let the Peace in my heart rule the day, I have a much better chance of being able to think clearly and sanely. Once my Heart and mind are working together, emotional stability replaces the chaos of daily life. If I follow this process through diligently each day, then the inner Peace that I find each morning begins to flow out of me and can spread around to the people, places and things all around me. The goal for today: Find inner Peace to create outer Peace! Have a great day, everybody!

JULY 9

Unselfish

"To be vital, faith must be accompanied by self-sacrifice and unselfish, constructive action."

For a long time I was praying and then waiting for God to take action and fix all of my problems for me. Now, I have a little better understanding of how this stuff works. I should pray ... then take action. Not just any action, but unselfish, constructive action. In other words, I should be asking God to give me what I need to be more helpful and useful to others. The goal for today: Help others—it is vital! Have a great day, everybody!

July 10

Overcome Fears

I didn't want to be alone ... but I had a fear of commitment. I didn't want to be told what to do ... but I had a fear of making my own decisions. I didn't want to run out of money ... but I had a fear of real work. I didn't want to be controlled ... but I had a fear of responsibility. I was one confused individual! Fortunately, there is a solution! The goal for today: Overcome my fears, commit intelligently, regain my self-esteem, earn my own keep and live within my means, embrace responsibility and live Free! Have a great day, everybody!

Right and Happy

I like the saying "Would you rather be right, or would you rather be happy?" but I've come to an interesting conclusion. I now believe that I can't claim to be Right, if I'm not Happy. "Right" and "Happy" are synonymous—you actually can't have one without the other. Even if the information that I'm giving you is accurate, that doesn't mean that my motive or attitude can't be wrong. Bottom line: if I'm unhappy, I'm wrong. The goal for today: Be Right and Happy because in reality it's impossible to just be one or the other! Have a great day, everybody!

I Don't Know Everything

What would be more foolish: not asking and doing it wrong, or asking and learning how to do it right? I was afraid to say "I don't know" because I was afraid that you would think I was stupid. I would pretend that I knew what I was doing, screw things up and then get defensive when someone would say, "I thought you said you knew how to do that." The goal for today: Be humble ... be logical ... admit it when I don't know... and remain teachable. The only thing that can make me look stupid is pretending that I know everything! Have a great day, everybody!

July 13

Breathe Deep

"He's alive, but feels absolutely nothing ... so is he?"
—Eddie Vedder

Yes, I woke up this morning. It could be worse. But it could be better, too, and that's what I want to strive for. I want to feel ... and I want to feel good! Not a superficial good ... not a drug or alcohol induced good ... but that feeling of being truly ALIVE! That state where nothing and no one can hurt me or bother me. The kind of good that you feel in the depths of your soul. The goal for today: Don't just breathe ... breathe deep of all the good that being alive has to offer! Have a great day everybody!

Rise Above Fear

"Fear isn't real ... the only place that fear can exist, is in our thoughts of the future." —From the movie After Earth

Take a minute to really think about that statement. It's simple, true and logical, yet it is one of the most profound and important insights that we will ever possess! Fear only exists in our minds, but if we let it hang out there long enough, then the things that we fear most, happen. WE begin to make them happen by giving them our attention. The goal for today: Think in the moment and rise above fear! Have a great day, everybody!

True Success in Life

I believe that unselfishness is the True sign of how well a person is REALLY doing. If you ask me how I'm doing and I tell you I'm doing great and spend the next ten minutes telling you about it and never think to ask you how you are doing, that means I'm selfish and self-centered and not doing anywhere near as well as I claim to be. Success comes directly from my desire to give freely of myself to others—primarily giving them Love. The goal for today: Have a genuine concern for the welfare of others and then I can claim True success in life! Have a great day, everybody!

July 16

Worthiness ... Equality ... and Forgiveness

I believe in myself today and I believe in you, too! I am finally beginning to understand that we are all created equal—I'm no better or worse than anyone else. There is no such thing as a bad person or an unworthy person. We are ALL good people who sometimes do bad things. This bad is always a temporary thing. I become good again as soon as I am truly sorry for what I've done and have an honest desire to do good again. The goal for today: Understand worthiness ... understand equality ... understand forgiveness ... and be good! Have a great day, everybody!

Survival

Self-preservation is human preservation! None of us could survive alone. Therefore, my REAL survival instinct should be geared toward the preservation of all. I should care about other people (even my enemies). I should care about the planet ... about natural resources ... sustainability ... and most importantly the condition we leave this world in for our children and grandchildren. The goal for today: Know that the best way to ensure my own survival is to help you ensure yours! Have a great day, everybody!

My Feelings Are Never Your Fault

"Say what you mean, but don't say it mean."

I have a better idea—if what I have to say could be mean, then I should change what I mean. Thinking mean things, but saying nice things, really just makes me a liar. Instead, I should do whatever it takes to get rid of the bad thoughts and feelings that I have toward anyone. If there aren't mean things going on inside of me. then mean things won't come out of me. The goal for today: Don't blame other people for my feelings and I won't ever have to worry about saying something mean! Have a great day, everybody!

I Promise ... I'm Sorry ...I Love You

There are three powerful, meaningful, terms that I've thrown around very lightly all of my life and they are "I promise" ... "I'm sorry" ... and "I love you." These are things that I should never say unless I mean it and in order to really mean it I must understand it. 1) *I promise* means I'm not just telling you what you want to hear, but in fact, I will keep my word. 2) *I'm sorry* means I won't do it again. I will stop repeating and apologizing. 3) *I love you* means that I am truly willing to give to you, looking for nothing in return. The goal for today: Understand it and mean it ... or don't say it! Have a great day, everybody!

July 20

Work With It ... Not Against It

"We chose to believe that our human intelligence was the last word, the alpha and the omega, the beginning and end of all. Rather vain of us, wasn't it?"

I can't create a planet and that means there's a Power greater than me. I don't understand all of existence and that means there's an Intelligence greater than me. It doesn't matter what I call it ... what matters is the attitude I take toward It and my willingness to work with It rather than against It. The goal for today: Sanely and logically work with this Powerful, Creative Intelligence ... instead of believing that I am it! Have a great day, everybody!

The Easy Way

There are two ways to learn the Truth. I can access it from within, through contemplation, or I can access it from without, through painful experience. When Sir Isaac Newton was asked how he discovered gravity he said "I thought about it... all the time." As a kid, I learned about gravity when I jumped off of a wall and came crashing down to the ground. There is an easy way and a hard way ... but either way I end up at the Truth. The goal for today: Think properly and learn a few lessons the easy way for a change! Have a great day, everybody!

You Can Never Care Too Much

"I care too much."

I've made this claim many times, but in reality, that's just silly. The Truth was that I had a fear of people not liking me, a fear of confrontation and a fear of being alone that caused me to be a doormat. I allowed people to walk all over me, take advantage of me and take me for granted because I was afraid. So the True statement would sound more like this: "I fear too much." The goal for today: Tell myself the real Truth ... get rid of fear and know that I can never care too much! Have a great day, everybody!

July 23

Be a Real Nice Guy

"Nice guys finish last." That's just not true. Being kind, considerate and polite while trying to manipulate people, doesn't make me a "nice guy." In order to actually be a nice guy, I have to be genuinely kind and loving. I have to be giving freely of myself to others. If I feel angry or hurt because you didn't show appreciation for my kindness, that is proof positive that it wasn't really kindness—it was in fact, fear based selfishness. The goal for today: If I want to avoid finishing last, I should learn how to really be a nice guy! Have a great day, everybody!

Rise Above Fear

There are a handful of things in this life that I am certain of and one of them is that fear is at the root of all my problems. My next thoughts, words and deeds will either be based on Love or fear ... and only I can decide which it will be. There was a time in my life that I would have disagreed with this statement, but now I can see that I had piled my fears so high and so wide that I could no longer see over or around them to the Truth. The goal for today: Tap into a Higher Power that will help me rise above my fear so I can see the Truth and start solving some problems! Have a great day, everybody!

July 25

Not Happy ... Not Natural

"It's human nature to get angry" (or any other negative emotion). That's just not true! It took many years to understand the difference between human nature and commonplace and I finally get it. Real human nature is a Purely positive influence ... a negative is never human nature! Just because everybody's doing it, doesn't mean it's normal and natural. That just means it's commonplace. The goal for today: Know that Happiness, Peace and Freedom are the natural order of things! Not happy ... not natural! Have a great day, everybody!

Find Some Facts

If I have an opinion that I feel strongly about I should try it out and prove to myself whether or not it's accurate. If my opinion proves itself, I can stop calling it an opinion. We have a different word for things that prove to be true—we call them facts. As I look around this troubled world, it seems that all our troubles come from trying to live by these unproven opinions. In fact, in a world governed by precise Laws and Principles, it is impossible to have a problem that is not caused by an opinion. The goal for today: Find some facts to live by! Have a great day everybody!

Real Peace Comes From Real Forgiveness

"Forgive others, not because they deserve forgive-ness, but because you deserve peace."

That is suggesting that pretend forgiveness can lead to real Peace. A genuine act of forgive-ness is the only way to get from anger to Peace. The fact of the matter is that if I'm not will-ing to genuinely forgive you, then I don't de-serve Peace. I'm not a big fan of these sayings that attempt to lift one person up by tearing another down. I guarantee you, this will not work. The goal for today: Know that real Peace comes from real forgiveness! Have a great day, everybody!

Wishing Bad Karma on You Brings Bad Karma on Me

"Karma is a bitch … I can't wait until you get yours."

I'm sure I've said this a time or two, but now I can see the absurdity of it. First of all, the law of karma doesn't need any enforcement help from me. It exists specifically so I don't have to play judge, jury and executioner. Secondly, me wishing bad karma on you would quite certainly be the best way to bring bad karma upon myself. The goal for today: Let the law of karma do its job and I'll do mine. And mine is to Love people … unconditionally! Have a great day, everybody!

July 29

Take Your Own Advice

The best way to help people is to teach them how to consult their own conscience. What does that mean? It means that the person with the problem already knows the solution— it's already inside of them. A method that I have found useful is to ask myself what I would tell you to do if you were having the same problem. Your solution is my solution. It's amazing how the Right answers come when we put ourselves in someone else's shoes. The goal for today: Know that what I would tell you to do, is exactly what I should do! Have a great day, everybody!

Nothing Feels Better

We have a best feeling and a worst feeling. My best feeling is when I am giving Love out freely to others, expecting nothing in return. Nothing feels better because that is our purpose for existing and what could feel better than fulfilling our intended purpose? My worst feeling is the fear of being alone. Nothing feels worse because it causes selfishness which destroys the opportunity to fulfill my intended purpose ... and what could possibly feel worse? The goal for today: Love ... because nothing feels better! Have a great day, everybody!

One Direction

I believe that real Love works kind of like electricity. It flows from the main, through the switch, out to the bulb. If it flows in the opposite direction—if the main is expected to get power back from the bulb, the house might burn down and then there would be no more electricity. I believe that Love also flows in one direction. It flows from God (or whatever you call the source), through our hearts, out into the world around us. The goal for today: I Love rather than trying to get Love! Have a great day everybody!

—

Fear Makes Everything Harder

"Relationships are hard work."

Well, they're not supposed to be! Love should be pretty free and easy if I'm doing it right. Some of my past relationships were hard work because I was full of fear. I was pretending to be someone I'm not and I was putting all sorts of conditions, stipulations and restrictions on people. If I'm with the wrong person (or I am the wrong person), the Law of Attraction will let me know. The goal for today: Know that life is only hard work, when I'm living it based on fear! Have a great day, everybody!

Don't Be Childish

If people mistreat me today, I will kill them with kindness. If people insult me today, I will genuinely give them Love in exchange. If people lie, cheat, or steal from me today, I will offer them forgiveness. I have come to the rock solid conclusion that treating people poorly because they treated me poorly first is childish and it is also the best way to guarantee my misery, as well as the other person's. The goal for today: Know that doing what's Right ... is always the Right thing to do! Have a great day, everybody!

Faith = Confidence

I have a lot of faith in God, but that won't get me very far if I have no confidence in myself to carry out His will. For example: I know God wants me to help people, but if I have myself convinced that I'm not good enough, then I can't do God's will. God's kingdom can't come and God's will can't be done in Earth as it is in Heaven unless I live up to my end of the bargain. The goal for today: Let my faith in God fill me full of the confidence in myself, which is required to carry out His perfect plan! Have a great day, everybody!

August 4

Give Love to Feel Love

"You must love yourself before you can love any-body else."

I don't believe that! We were built to GIVE Love and therefore, it is impossible to Love myself unless I give Love freely out to others. Love, by definition, is something that can only be felt or experienced by giving. We are all born with a heart full of Love and the reason we exist is to manifest or press outward this Love. What better way to Love myself than to fulfill my intended purpose? The goal for to-day: Love others to Love myself! Have a great day, everybody!

AUGUST 5

Strive for Perfection ... Be Grateful for Progress

"We claim progress, not perfection" but "Don't rest on your laurels."

These two quotes, properly combined, are a powerful formula for daily life.

1. Says forward progress is the key to happiness and success.
2. Says that striving for perfection is the key to forward progress.

Striving for perfection is the best way to achieve forward progress and keep from resting on my laurels (or being inactive, the enemy of progress). Is perfection attainable? I don't know ... but I'm sure as hell going to try today! Have a great day, everybody!

AUGUST 6

~

Soar High

"No bird soars too high if he soars with his own wings." —William Blake

I was once told that I overcame a problem too quickly?!? There is no such thing as solving a problem too quickly, but there is such a thing as leaning too heavily on someone else's strength as the solution. The Right way to help each other is to encourage each other to help ourselves. The goal for today: Don't wait another day. Rise above our problems on our wings ... the wings of Strength, Courage and Wisdom that exist deep down inside of every one of us! Have a great day, everybody!

Giving Just Feels Good

Think back to the happiest moment of your life. I would be willing to wager that the happiest moments of all of our lives were moments when we were giving, rather than getting. Giving just feels good, especially when we give something other than money. It's easy to give money, but that doesn't feel the same as giving Love to a child ... an elder ... a sibling or a friend. Those genuine, face-to-face acts of kindness are what really matter! The goal for today: Do what makes us feel best, more frequently! Have a great day, everybody!

August 8

"It's Not OK"

"I'm having a bad day" is not a good enough reason for me to mistreat people. I have been guilty of this many, many times in life. I have a bad day, treat you like garbage and think that saying "I'm sorry, I'm just having a bad day" makes everything OK. It's not OK to treat people poorly because I'm having a bad day. It doesn't matter how tragic my day is—that still does not give me the right to treat you poorly. The goal for today: If I'm having a bad day, I should fix it, not take it out on others! Have a great day, everybody!

Be Exceptional ... Just Like Everybody Else

I was talking to a friend who said she used to be very troubled by the thought of being average. We are all average... that's kind of the point of being created equal. Created equal doesn't mean we will all have the same amount of money or the same physical qualities, it means equal at heart. The only thing that makes us average is that we are created equal ... but if you really stop and think about it, we are all equally exceptional. The goal for today: Be exceptional—just like everybody else! Have a great day everybody!

‡

Ask Him Yourself

"God works through people."

I don't disagree with this... however, I was using it as a copout because I was afraid to think for myself and be responsible for my own decisions. I should not be irresponsible ... I should not be blindly led ... and I certainly should not expect God to work through everybody except me. The goal for today: Know that it's not my job to tell you what God wants you to do—it's my job to help you get to know God, so you can ask Him yourself! Have a great day, everybody!

~

Judgment

I'm only afraid that people are passing negative judgment on me when I'm doing something that I believe in my heart is wrong. It is actually my negative judgment of myself that is making me feel that way—not the judgment of others. I don't fear the judgment of others when I'm not doing anything wrong. The goal for today: Overcome fear ... stop doing what I know I shouldn't being doing and then the judgment of others cannot affect me. Have a great day, everybody!

In Your Own Heart

I have a friend who THINKS that he doesn't believe in God, but he does. He is a decent human being, a responsible adult, a hard worker, he's kind and respectful, he's a single father and a damn good one! What he doesn't believe in is the conception of God that was impressed upon him earlier in life, either by society, or by an organized religion. He is a good man, a Godly man, whether he knows it or not. The goal for today: Don't lose faith in God because of someone else's belief system doesn't work for me. Find the Truth in my own heart and live Free! Have a great day, everybody!

August 13

Revisit the Truth ... Don't Rewrite It

The instructions on how to be successful at life work just like any other instructions. Example: If I buy a desk and the manual says "Using the wooden dowels provided, attach part A to part B" and I decide to use scotch tape instead, I'm not going to get the Right results. It may appear to have worked until later on when I place something on that shelf and it comes crashing down. The only way to guarantee the Right results is to follow the instructions, not make up my own as I go along. The goal for today: Follow the instructions and if it goes wrong, revisit the instructions—don't rewrite them! Have a great day, everybody!

August 14

Refuse to Go Without

If I'm depressed, should I pretend I'm not—find someone or something to blame—or fix it? If I'm anxious, should I pretend I'm not—find someone or something to blame— or fix it? If I'm angry or hurt or feeling insecure, should I pretend I'm not—find someone to blame—or fix it? I know that many of you are thinking "easier said than done," but it is actually infinitely easier to fix it, than it is to live with it day in and day out, year after year. I've been there. The goal for today: There is always a solution and I refuse to go without it! Have a great day, everybody!

August 15

Good Is Always God's Plan

"In God's time, not ours"

I don't disagree, but this has been grossly misinterpreted by many (including me). There's no such thing as time in God's world. Time is a man-made invention. God only exists in the present moment, not in the past (depression), nor in the future (anxiety). So, if good isn't happening to me right here and now, it's because I'm not living in the present, not because God is withholding good from me. The goal for today: Know that good is always God's plan—24/7! Have a great day, everybody!

Break the Cycle

When people are afraid, they act poorly (God knows I did). If I can understand that it's fear and not take it personally, I can avoid anger and frustration. Fear is an illness. It's not necessarily a physical disorder (although it may cause one), but it is a soul sickness that manifests itself in all sorts of ugly ways. Fear causes dishonesty ... dishonesty causes selfishness ... selfishness causes resentment and this becomes a vicious cycle. The goal for today: Get rid of fear. Break the vicious cycle and find some Peace, Happiness and Freedom! Have a great day, everybody!

Second Nature

"If you don't control your subconscious mind, it will control you and you'll call it fate." —Carl Jung

Do you have any idea what is going on in the back of your mind right now? I never did. Not controlling my subconscious contributed to my so-called accidents ... my insomnia ... my anxiety and depression. It wreaks havoc on us when we are unaware of its involvement in our daily lives. The goal for today: Make a habit of having positive thoughts, as often as possible, and keep doing it until it becomes subconscious or second nature. Have a great day, everybody!

August 18

Real Bliss

Ignorance isn't really bliss. Ignoring my problems won't fix them or bring about happiness. We all have a different threshold for emotional pain and ignorance, or unknowing, is a big factor in it. If I honestly don't know that what I'm doing is wrong, then the emotional price isn't as painful. However, once I start knowingly doing wrong, the pain becomes too much and I am forced to take action ... good, bad or otherwise. The goal for today: Experience real bliss by knowing what's Right and doing it! Have a great day, everybody!

Learn ... Grow ... Help Others

I'm not always in the best situation, but I can always make the best of every situation. We all have our problems and that will never change. It's how we react to them and how we let them affect us that really matters. I try to use my troubles as a guide to progress—an opportunity to learn and grow. Learning how to face and overcome adversity is absolutely essential to our Lives and Happiness! The goal for today: Make the best of EVERY situation by diligently seeking out opportunities to be helpful to others! Have a great day, everybody!

God is a Pretty Good Therapist

"There is nothing that can be done by any form of psychotherapy that cannot be better done by the Practice of the Presence of God." —Emmet Fox

I spent years trying to get rid of my anxiety and depression and failed. Then one day someone asked me if I created the world and at that moment, the realization that there must be something more powerful than human beings crept into my mind and changed EVERYTHING! The goal for today: Never underestimate the Healing Power that exists deep down inside of each and every one of us! Have a great day, everybody!

You're Number One

"Look out for number one."

We are desperately in need of understanding when it comes to sayings like this. The human heart was specifically designed to feel its best when it is giving freely of itself to others—nothing feels better. Therefore, the best way to look out for number one is to intelligently put the welfare of others ahead of my own. The goal for today: Make sure that the person right in front of me, that needs my help, is number one! Have a great day, everybody!

Keep Up the Good Work

"If everything seems right, then there is definitely something wrong."

That's just crazy! Maybe the reason that nothing good ever seems to last is because I keep filling myself full of fear and doubt—destroying hope, with negative, derogatory thoughts like that one. It's time to rise above our own defeatist attitudes and believe that things can get and stay good, so long as we keep up the good work. The goal for today: Keep thinking and doing good and things can and will stay Right! Have a great day, everybody!

Where I'm Really Supposed to Be

"You're right where you're supposed to be."

I have been told this in the midst of struggles and difficulties and could never understand why I was "supposed to be" miserable. Now I know that I was confused about it because I was NOT where I was supposed to be. I'm supposed to be happy, joyous and free and if I'm not, I should work toward correcting it and strive to get to that better place. The goal for today: Do whatever it takes to get to where I'm really supposed to be—Happy, Helpful and Alive! Have a great day, everybody!

Seek ... Find ... and Follow

To not believe in a Creator is to believe that I was not created. I'm sure we all believe that something created us, or we wouldn't be here. Whatever I choose to believe created me, turns out to be my God. I believe in a higher intelligence, because if human intelligence were the highest, we would already know everything, which clearly is not the case. The goal for today: Open my mind to the fact that there is a force out there that can and will make my life better if I seek, find and follow it! Have a great day, everybody!

Don't Default to Bad

Why do we tend to think the worst of ourselves? If someone doesn't treat me right, should I assume that it's because I'm no good? Or is it possible that they are having a bad day and happened to take it out on me? If I take it personally, I feel bad about myself, hurt and maybe even angry. If I don't take it personally, I can be kind, compassionate and understanding. The goal for today: Don't default to low self-esteem. See things for what they really are and fill my day with Peace, Contentment and Helpfulness! Have a great day, everybody!

AUGUST 26

Early and Often

The most important thing to ask of God on a daily basis is that He direct my thinking. If I have a problem, He will direct my thinking to the solution. If I need something, He will direct my thinking to what I need to do to get it. If other people are in need, He will direct my thinking to how I can help them. If I'm full of fear and anxiety, He will direct it to Peace and Contentment. If I'm full of anger and frustration, He will direct it to Love and Harmony. The goal for today: Ask God to direct my thinking, early and often. Have a great day, everybody!

Would You Rather Feel Good or Bad?

Why does it feel so good to help people? Because it's the Right thing to do. Why doesn't it feel good to hurt people? Because it's the wrong thing to do. All I have to do to KNOW if I'm doing the Right thing is pay attention to the feeling that comes from doing it. The catch is to fully understand that that spiteful, vindictive, twisted sense of pleasure, that we seem to get from hurting people, isn't real. The goal for today: Know the difference between real happiness and rotten happiness and live according to the one I would rather feel. Have a great day, everybody!

=

Like Attracts Like

If I want to be loved ... I must be loving. If I want to be understood ... I must be understanding. If I want to be respected ... I must be respectful. If I want to be forgiven ... I must be forgiving. It would be crazy of me to believe that I could be an angry, miserable, intolerant, disrespectful jerk and expect to be surrounded by people who are kind, considerate, patient, tolerant and loving. The goal for today: Remember that one of the all-embracing Master Laws of Life says that "Like Attracts Like!" Have a great day, everybody!

Clear ... Concise ... and Conscious

My problems are the result of selfishness, dishonesty resentment and fear. My solutions are the result of Selflessness, Honesty, Love and Purity. All life is a paradox. I can't help myself, except by helping others. Admitting that I've lied, is Honest. The only way to stop hate, is with Love. Fear will cause the things I'm most afraid to happen. The goal for today: Understand the paradox, live in reality and experience Life the way it was intended to be. Be clear, be concise and be consciously aware! Have a great day, everybody!

If It's Me I Can Fix It

"And if there's something you'd like to do… just let me continue to blame you." —Footsteps *by Pearl Jam*

This is a song about spending my whole life blaming everybody else for all of my problems, just to wake up one day and realize that it was nobody's fault but mine. The day I admitted I was my problem was the day I began to heal. Taking responsibility is now a very important part of my daily life. If it's you, I can't fix it; if it's me, I can. The goal for today: Know that personal responsibility leads to personal freedom! Have a great day, everybody!

The Easy Way

"They never said it would be easy... they said it would be worth it."

Is it easier to Love ... or hate? Is it easier to be Honest ... or to live a lie? Is it easier to Give ... or take? Is it easier to make decisions based on Purity ... or fear? The Right way is always the easiest way! Living Right is easy. The only thing that is hard about it is the breaking of old, bad habits that I've practiced for years. The goal for today: Practice living the Right way and it will become the easy way and it is definitely worth it! Have a great day, everybody!

September 1

Get Rid of It

A few days ago, I talked about asking God to direct my thinking and here is the interesting part of that: God will NEVER direct my thinking to a negative. He will never direct it to things like fear, anger, worry, remorse, selfishness, dishonesty, criticism, revenge, etc., etc. If I ask God to direct my thinking and actually allow it to happen, I am guaranteed to have a more positive and productive day. The goal for today: If I have a negative thought, know that it didn't come from God and get rid of it! Have a great day, everybody!

Know the Truth

We live in a dishonest world. Everywhere we turn we see distortions of the truth—some out of selfishness, some out of fear and stills others out of ignorance. Most of my life I had trust issues as the result of people's lies, but I have since found the solution. I now realize that I don't have trust issues because of people's lies; I have trust issues because I'm unwilling to do whatever it takes to find the Truth. The goal for today: Don't be blindly led. Know the Truth, whether anyone is speaking it or not! Have a great day, everybody!

September 3

Turn My Brain Off

"I wish I could turn my brain off."

I've thought this a million times, but do I really want to be mindless? Do I really want to not think or feel? There is a better way! When my mind torments me, it's because I'm not using it properly, not because a working brain is a bad thing to have. I can choose my thoughts, so if I can't sleep at night, should I take a pill or choose better thoughts? The goal for today: Focus on the task at hand—breathe easy and don't let my mind run roughshod on me! Have a great day, everybody!

SEPTEMBER 4

Love and Service

"Time heals all wounds."

That may be true of some physical injuries, but not so with mental and emotional wounds. If I fear being alone and my girl leaves me, time may give me a chance to go find a new girl and pretend that I no longer have that fear, but it won't heal the wound. The fear will continue to exist for all time, until I deal with it properly. I may be smiling, but if my new girl leaves, I go right back to being afraid—I've solved nothing. The goal for today: Know that Love and Service are our real healing qualities! Have a great day, everybody!

Healthy Respect

"Sometimes fear is healthy."

There is a big difference between acting out of fear and acting out of respect. The term "healthy fear" is an oxymoron. There is no such thing ... anything built on fear will eventually fail. On the other hand, having a "healthy respect" for a potentially dangerous situation is a really good idea. Should I do what's Right because I'm terrified, or because I respect myself, others and God? The goal for today: Get rid of fear. Learn and teach how to stay safe the Right way—through a healthy respect! Have a great day, everybody!

Demonstrate the Truth

"Sometimes it is better not to tell the truth."

Lying is never the Right thing to do. Anything built on a lie will eventually fall apart. There is a big difference between lying to spare someone's feelings and speaking the Truth with tact and common sense. I don't go out of my way to beat people over the head with the Truth, but I'm not going to lie to them either. The goal for today: Know that if I demonstrate the Truth in my daily life, I won't have to browbeat anybody with it—they'll come asking for it! Have a great day, everybody!

Helping Others Helps Everybody

"That's good selfishness."

There is absolutely no such thing as "good selfishness!" Taking care of my own life is called responsibility, not selfishness. When I put my needs ahead of yours, nothing good comes out of it. I have an obligation to get my life in order and put the effort into keeping it that way, but I have a far greater obligation to Love my neighbor ... to Love my enemies ... to Love everyone! None of us can do this on our own—we need to help each other! The goal for today: Know that helping others helps everybody! Have a great day, everybody!

Free of Anger

"I have a right to be angry."

In reality, there is no such thing as justifiable anger. Anger is born of selfishness and is always wrong. It is also a definite sign of a lack of understanding. I get mad at people because I fail to realize that they are acting the way they are acting because they are having their own problems. I don't like the way anger feels anymore and if it does crop up, I want to get rid of it as quickly as possible. The goal for today: Live free of anger by understanding and helping others! Have a great day, everybody!

An Honest Effort

The past four days, I talked about how selfishness, resentment, dishonesty and fear are not OK. I don't practice this perfectly, but I don't justify it either. I am no longer under the delusion that it's OK to engage in them. If I spent half as much time trying to correct these defects as I have trying to justify them, I would have a much better chance of finding Happiness and Peace. The goal for today: Know that these things are wrong and put an honest effort into doing the opposite: Purity, Honesty, Selflessness and Love! Have a great day, everybody!

Avoid Apologies

"Never apologize for being yourself."

This is not a free pass to run around treating people poorly and claim its OK because I'm just "being me." If I'm acting like an ass, then I should change myself and I may owe a few apologies. Properly understood, this saying is suggesting that if I'm living the Right way, no apologies will be necessary. I only say I'm sorry when I believe I've done something wrong. The goal for today: Speak the Truth and treat people Right, because being a good person is the best way to avoid having to make apologies! Have a great day, everybody!

September 11

Fix Myself

"Everybody just needs to vent."

This is a dangerous statement! Getting something off my chest may bring some temporary relief, but it will do more harm than good in the long run, unless I'm venting in an honest attempt to spot, admit and correct my own mistakes. Just venting about my problems actually gives them more power against me. It's like throwing another log on the fire, wondering why it won't go out. The goal for today: Vent properly—to fix myself, rather than tarnish others! Have a great day, everybody!

⇌

We Choose Our Thoughts

Is it impossible to have a positive thought right now ... or am I thinking negatively by choice? Our thinking is always our choice! If I don't want to feel angry or scared or depressed or anxious or unworthy, I don't have to—I can change my thoughts. When I was first told that it sounded crazy, I didn't know I could control my mind. I thought it controlled me. The goal for today: Regain control of my life by regaining control of my mind (I ask God to direct my thinking), because once the mind is Right, the emotions and actions will follow! Have a great day, everybody!

The Right Expectation

"If I have no expectations, I never get let down."

Yeah, but I never get lifted up either! I try to have realistic expectations. For example: I don't expect people who are living the wrong way to do the Right thing. I expect them to do the wrong thing, and with the Right expectation I can keep myself out of harm's way and maybe even help people change their ways (if they are willing). The goal for today: Don't get rid of expectations ... learn how to have the Right expectations and watch things turn out exactly as they should! Have a great day, everybody!

September 14

Make the Right Ones

"Everything happens for a reason."

Another saying that I agree with but completely misunderstood and was using as a cop-out. Everything does happen for a reason. Good things happen when we think, feel and act the Right way; bad things happen when we think, feel and act the wrong way. This is very simple stuff, but for some reason it took me thirty years to get it. The goal for today: Know that our decisions are what make things happen and ask God to help us make the Right ones! Have a great day, everybody!

SEPTEMBER 15

Sense of Worth

I don't need a pat on the back to feel good about myself. I don't need others to validate my worth. I'm not going to feel worthless if someone doesn't return the Love, helping hand, or favors I give out. My sense of worth comes from inside—not outside. Any good feeling I get from outside is temporary, but the way it feels in my heart when I do the Right thing, for the Right reason, is where my real sense of worth comes from. The goal for today: Think, feel and act properly toward others and feel my sense of worth steadily increase! Have a great day, everybody!

Break the Chains

We become slaves to the things that we are afraid to admit to others. When I screw up and I'm afraid of what people will think of me if they find out, I become paranoid. I'm looking over my shoulder. I'm waiting for the other shoe to drop— my every thought and action, at times, is built around this fear and it makes my life incredibly uncomfortable. The goal for today: Break the chains ... face my fears ... admit my mistakes ... teach others how to do the same ... and live Free! Have a great day, everybody!

Be Hard on Yourself

"Don't be too hard on yourself."

I'm of the opposite belief! If I'm not happy, I'm doing something wrong, and although we all make mistakes, that doesn't mean that I should go easy on myself. I hold myself to a high standard and when I fall short, I put effort into fixing it, rather than using "everybody makes mistakes" to justify it and continue to do it. The goal for today: Hold myself to a high moral standard and constructively criticize myself on a regular basis in an attempt to be a better person. Have a great day, everybody!

Want to Hear the Truth

Do you want me to help you, or do you want me to tell you you're right? I'm not a big fan of telling people what they want to hear. I'd rather encourage people to want to hear the Truth. For some reason we seem opposed to the Truth. We have all heard "the truth will set you free," but we don't really believe it. I have come to the conclusion that the only way to help people is to tell them the Truth. The goal for today: Don't lie … help the willing see the Truth and help the unwilling by not helping. Have a great day, everybody!

Be Set Free

Yesterday I mentioned that "the Truth will set you free," but the real question is ... free from what? It will set me free from fear—the Truth says fear isn't real. It will set me free from dishonesty—the Truth eliminates the need to lie to myself or others. It will set me free from selfishness—I will not grab for more of everything, because if I have the Truth, I have all that is worth having. It will set me free from resentment—the Truth tells me that anger is ALWAYS wrong. The goal for today: Be set free! Have a great day, everybody!

Kind to Everyone

I don't know who coined the phrase "kill them with kindness," but I absolutely love it! I've tried it, and it works! Sometimes it takes time but if I stay persistent, it always pans out in the end. It's hard to stay mad at someone who is being nice to you. There is a catch, however—it must be sincere to have any real, lasting effects. People can tell the difference between a genuine act of kindness and a sarcastic, fake smile. The goal for today: Be kind to everyone, no matter what ... because that's the way that I would want to be treated! Have a great day, everybody!

SEPTEMBER 21

Freedom of Religion

Someone once suggested to me that I choose my own conception of God because the conception I had before came from someone else and was not working. This is what I came up with: God is omnipotent (all powerful) and omnipresent (always present) ... caring and helpful ... kind and loving ... understanding and forgiving ... patient and tolerant. God is fair and just ... honest and omniscient (all knowing) ... strength and direction ... God is the light in the darkness. The goal for today: Choose Freedom of religion! Have a great day, everybody!

It's Harder to Live With Fear

It's not always easy to face our fears, but it's a hell of a lot harder to live with them. Fear is the driving force behind all of my problems and I need to learn how to cope with it. Admitting when I'm wrong ... facing people that I've hurt ... being alone ... these fears can be debilitating at times. But, when I really stop and think about it, I can see that not facing them is far more debilitating and potentially destructive. The goal for today: Spot, admit and correct my fears so I can stop drowning in them! Have a great day, everybody!

⌐

Find the Facts

We are divided by opinions when we should be unified by facts. It is my responsibility as a family member, a friend, a co-worker, an adult, or simply as a human being to know the difference between a fact and an opinion and live my life in accordance with the facts. Opinions divide us; they cause arguments, squabbles, confrontations and even wars. If opinions were accurate, we wouldn't call them opinions—we would call them facts. The goal for today: Find the facts, at all costs, because we can't stand united without them! Have a great day, everybody!

Every Heart and Soul

There is only one place to get inner peace: from within. There is a powerful source of peace deep down inside of every man, woman and child. I call it God, but regardless of what I call it, I must get in touch with it if I want peace, for there is no other source. I can't get it through money, women, things, vacations, drugs, alcohol, or any other source outside of myself. The goal for today: Seek, find and follow that Peace, Power and Direction that exists deep down inside of every heart and soul! Have a great day, everybody!

My Own Beliefs

I can't build my life based on your beliefs. Not only is it a bad idea to blindly follow the beliefs of others, but it's actually impossible. Anything that I've been taught that I don't truly believe, in my own heart, will fade away eventually. It is impossible to build a belief system on things that I don't believe. The goal for today: Know that the most important thing for me to do is to search my own heart and find out what I really believe, because Peace and Happiness never come from begrudgingly following someone else's beliefs and ideas. Have a great day, everybody!

Thinking Controls Behavior

"You are a product of your environment."

It doesn't have to be that way! We have all seen cases where people came from bad environments and turned out just fine. We've also seen cases where people came from good environments and turned out screwed up. The fact of the matter is that although our environment may sway our behavior, it cannot govern our behavior. The goal for today: Know that my environment doesn't control my behavior— my own thinking does! Have a great day, everybody!

⇁

Seek ... Find ... and Follow

The Truth will set you free! I recently spoke with someone who claimed to believe something that she didn't really believe. She made this claim because she was afraid I would judge her, but I saw through the lie and I didn't judge her. Once she saw that they couldn't lie to me and that I wasn't going to judge her, she started telling the Truth and I watched her eyes light up and hope reenter her heart. The goal for today: Help each other seek, find and follow the Truth, because our Happiness and Freedom depend upon it! Have a great day, everybody!

September 28

For Them!

"It is not strange ... to mistake change for progress."
—Millard Fillmore

We have made many changes over the past 75 years or so, but very few of them have brought about a change for the better ... very few could claim forward progress. I believe that we need to change back to the Principles that this country was founded on to begin with. The goal for today: Life, Liberty, Freedom, Justice, Peace, Prosperity and most importantly Posterity (future generations)—we need to get it right for them! Have a great day, everybody!

Except God

It's never anybody else's fault that I am annoyed. Sometimes the things people do annoy me, other times they don't. That is proof positive that I am in control of my own feelings. They are not being forced on me from the outside by people, places or things. When my head is screwed on straight, I don't let other people control my feelings, my moods, or my sense of worth. The goal for today: Know that my thoughts are mine ... my feelings are mine and my actions are mine ... and don't relinquish control of them to anyone except God! Have a great day, everybody!

Want the Truth

If I don't know the Truth about something, it's because I don't want it. The only thing that can keep me from the Truth is my own laziness and or fear. I'm not willing to do the work to find it, or I'm afraid of what knowing it will require of me. It's actually a lot less work to live by the Truth than it is to live a lie and nothing bad can ever happen as a result of the Truth! The goal for today: Go get the Truth. We have a lot left to learn, but there is nothing that can't be known! Have a great day, everybody!

A Genuine Concern

It is impossible to be unhappy without first being selfish. This is true simply because it would be impossible for me to know that I was unhappy, unless of course, I was thinking about myself at that moment. When I become aware that I am unhappy, I should instantly start looking for someone to help or to care about. If it's 3:00 a.m. and no one's around ... then I should at least think about helping others. The goal for today: Have a genuine concern for the welfare of others and be happy! Have a great day, everybody!

October 2

It's Time to Grow Up

As kids we are all taught these three things: Sticks and stones may break my bones, but names will never hurt me. Two wrongs don't make a right. If all your friends jump off a bridge would you do it too? Now, I have to ask myself: Do I still let name calling hurt me? Do I still wrong people because they wronged me first? Do I still do stupid stuff that I know I shouldn't do because everybody's doing it? I carried these childish things out, way too far into adulthood and it's time for me to grow up. The goal for today: Act like an adult! Have a great day, everybody!

October 3

Don't Choose Anything Else

Are you happy right now, at this very moment? If you answered "yes" then good for you—you must be doing something right. If you answered "no" then I suggest you change your mind ... for after all, happiness is a choice. Before you say to yourself "Easier said than done" or 'I wish it was that easy" just try it—you might be pleasantly surprised to find that it is that simple. The goal for today: Choose happiness ... because it wouldn't make sense to choose anything else! Have a great day, everybody!

OCTOBER 4

Help Them Properly

"For the type of person who is able and willing to get well, little charity, in the ordinary sense of the word, is needed or wanted."

There are three types of people in the world. There is the type who are able and willing ... they simply get pointed in the right direction. There's the type who are able but unwilling ... they get prayers and my help, if or when, they become willing. There's the type who are willing but legitimately unable ... they get everything I've got to give. The goal for today: Know who I'm dealing with so I can help them properly! Have a great day, everybody!

October 5

The Truth Is Simple

The Truth is buried so far down, under mountains of theories and opinions, that we have completely lost sight of it. I've spent the past decade or so, searching and digging, finding bits and pieces of it and trying to reconstruct it … and what I've found to this point, is amazing! It was so hard to find because I was looking for something complex and mysterious, but the Truth turns out to be simplicity at its finest. The goal for today: Follow my Heart … Live in the moment … Love my neighbor and be Happy! Have a great day, everybody!

October 6

Most Important

People can deceive me when my thinking is self-centered. If I'm paying more attention to me than you, I will miss all the signs that tell me whether or not people are telling me the truth. Every day, many times each day, I try to remind myself that helping others is the most important thing to do in life. And the best way to help others is to pay attention to them, which can only be done by paying less attention to myself. The goal for today: Ask God to help me not be selfish, because I can't help you, if all I'm thinking about is me! Have a great day, everybody!

OCTOBER 7

They Are Mine

If I told you that you're smart, beautiful and have a great personality, would you believe me? If I told you that you're stupid, ugly and boring, would you believe me? Why do we have a tendency to only believe the bad things people say about us? And furthermore, if you can't force me to feel good about myself, why am I convinced that you can force me to feel bad about myself? The goal for today: Reclaim control of my feelings and emotions, good, bad or otherwise ... after all, they are mine! Have a great day, everybody!

OCTOBER 8

Imagination and Meaning

"Your imagination will be fired. Life will mean something at last."

I once believed "You're born, you pay taxes and you die." No meaning ... no imagination. But I have found a way of life that is full of meaning and definitely has my imagination fired! This way of life has been passed on from generation to generation for thousands of years and the more I practice it, the more meaning my life has. The goal for today: Don't let life get boring and pointless ... imagination makes anything possible and helping others gives life great meaning! Have a great day, everybody!

OCTOBER 9

Properly Cope With Fear

Most of my life I claimed that I was not afraid of anything, but that claim itself is proof of fear. I was afraid to admit I was afraid. In my mind, fear was a sign of weakness, so I had to hide it from the world at all costs. Everybody is faced with fear from time to time and denying it won't make it go away. Admitting it and working through it is the Right way to cope with fear. I can't fix it, without first admitting it. The goal for today: Cope with my fears properly and they will become fewer and fewer as time passes! Have a great day, everybody!

Nothing Feels Better ...
Nothing Feels Worse

I was driving home from work one night hating myself and my life when my phone rang. The call was from a friend in need. I spent at least half an hour trying to help him solve his problem and by the time I got off the phone, I felt pretty good about myself and my life. We were put here to help each other and therefore ... nothing could feel better! To disregard the well-being of others is to defeat our intended purpose and therefore ... nothing could feel worse! The goal for today: Do what I was put here to do! Have a great day, everybody!

OCTOBER 11

I Took Responsibility

Every human being chooses his or her path. One path leads to happiness and one path leads to misery. No one can force any of us to choose one path or the other ... this is a choice that can ONLY be made by the individuals themselves. I got to a point in life where I had to stop claiming that people, places, things or maybe God Himself put me on the wrong path. Once I took responsibility, I was able to correct my mistakes and get back on the Right path. The goal for today: Be responsible and learn to choose Right! Have a great day, everybody!

October 12

Help People Find Solutions

If I need to know the square root of 144 and I don't know how to figure it out, what would you say? A) I can relate ... I had that problem before, too. Or B) A square can be found by multiplying the square root number by itself. Example: 10x10=100—that's too low ... 11x11=122—still too low ...12x12=144—there it is. It's great that we can all "relate" to each other's problems, but wouldn't it be even better if we could help solve each other's problems? The goal for today: Help people find answers, because there is always a solution! Have a great day, everybody!

October 13

A Mustard Seed

With just a mustard seed of faith, we can accomplish some incredibly positive, constructive, amazing things! Unfortunately ... a mustard seed of doubt can do the same thing in the opposite direction. I've been on both sides of this fence and the grass is definitely always greener on the faith side of it and that's where I want to stay. The goal for today: Have faith in God ... have faith in myself ... have faith in others ... because working together, we can move mountains! Have a great day, everybody!

OCTOBER 14

⌖

The Only Real Solution

"All causation is mental." —Emmet Fox

What the hell does that mean? It means that everything that has ever happened, in the history of mankind, happened in someone's mind first! All of the problems that we are faced with in the world today are a direct result of wrong thinking. For example: Is it a good idea to drink and drive? Of course not! Why do people do it? Because they aren't thinking clearly. The goal for today: Learn how to think properly ... because it is the only REAL solution to any problem! Have a great day, everybody!

Have the Right Thought

"Think before you speak."

I agree, but there's a catch. We always think before we speak ... actually, it's impossible to speak without thinking first. The catch is to have the Right thought before I speak. If I think: "It's your fault I feel this way," I'm bound to say something foolish and inaccurate. If I think "It's dishonest of me to believe that you can make me feel," I've got a better chance of saying something sane and honest. The goal for today: Don't just think before I speak ... have the Right thought before I speak! Have a great day, everybody!

October 16

People Need My Help ... Not My Anger

"I only get angry at you because I care."

I'm sorry, but that's just not true. I get angry because things aren't going "my" way. Only selfishness can lead to anger ... not because I said so, but because it is a Universal Law of Life. I can only get angry when I believe that I am going to be negatively affected by someone else's actions or decisions. The goal for today: Tell myself the Truth about my anger so I can overcome it and be genuinely helpful to the troubled soul that needs my help—not my anger! Have a great day, everybody!

Money ... Titles ... and Test Scores

Just because people come from a good home, or have financial security or a high IQ, doesn't necessarily mean they have it all together and are happy. I know because I was one of them. But the selfish lifestyle that I was living trumped all of the good that I grew up in. Money, titles and test scores aren't the deciding factors in whether or not we are good people—how we treat people is. The goal for today: Have a genuine concern for the welfare of others ... because that's what matters most! Have a great day, everybody!

October 18

Deep Down Inside

"I'm not strong enough."

Someone said to me, "I don't think I'm strong enough to handle this on my own," and I said, "You're not ... neither am I and neither is anyone else." We all have a source of Power deep down inside of ourselves. It doesn't matter if you call it God or inner strength or whatever other name you choose to give it—it's there. The goal for today: Tap into this Power, stay connected to it on a daily basis, and utilize it to solve my problems and yours! Have a great day, everybody!

OCTOBER 19

Don't Set Standards for Others

"We spoke of intolerance while we were intolerant ourselves."

If I had a nickel for every time I bitched about somebody doing something that I had been guilty of doing many times myself, I'd be rich. I get mad when people lie, as if I've never lied. I get mad when people are selfish, as if I've never been selfish. I expect you to understand me, when I'm unwilling to try to understand you. The goal for today: Stop setting standards for others to live up to and start practicing personal responsibility instead! Have a great day, everybody!

OCTOBER 20

Opportunity

The attitude I take toward something or someone will dictate the affect that it has on me. If I hate my job, I will be unhappy doing it. If I constantly find fault with my girlfriend, I will have an unhappy relationship. Even the weather can make me miserable if I let it—but only if I let it. The goal for today: View a job as an opportunity to help people. View my girlfriend as an opportunity to give Love. Do my best to take a positive attitude into all my affairs and be happy! Have a great day, everybody!

~

Live and Let Live

"Attraction rather than promotion"

Someone once said to me, "You better believe!" and I basically said, "Go f*** yourself!" Years later someone said to me, "Why don't you choose your own conception of God?" and I said, "That's a great idea! Can you help me?" Forcing my beliefs on people will drive them further away. Demonstrating my beliefs will draw people in. The goal for today: Live it ... don't push it or sell it or try to scare people into it! Freedom of Religion! Have a great day, everybody!

OCTOBER 22

This Simple Formula

"Trust God, clean house, help others."

The three things that matter most to me are, my relationship with God, which is an active one. I don't just call on God when I have a problem. My willingness to see the Truth, which means knowing that if I'm disturbed ... there is something wrong with me. And my Honest desire to help others, which is the best way to keep my own life in order. The goal for today: Follow this simple formula to a Peaceful, Contented, Useful Life! Have a great day, everybody!

OCTOBER 23

A Real Leader

A real leader doesn't tell people what to do ... he teaches them what to do. When I was trying get my life in order, I found one of those *real* leaders. He didn't fix my problems for me, he didn't bark orders from his pedestal, and he didn't demand that I bow to him. He introduced me to a better way of life, if I cared to have it. He taught me how to help myself and encouraged me to follow my own conscience. Then he suggested that I go out and become a leader myself. The goal for today: Be a real leader and really help people! Have a great day, everybody!

October 24

Clearly ... Thoroughly ... Unconditionally

We are all at different levels of understanding in life and that's why it's so important for me to learn how to communicate with people in a clear and simple manner. Even when the topic is complex, the communication doesn't have to be. God is a complex thing to talk about, but if we stick to the basics, listen to one another and keep our egos in check, we can find common ground. The goal for today: Communicate clearly ... understand thoroughly ... and Love unconditionally! Have a great day, everybody!

Not So Different After All

Imagine what life might be like if everyone openly and honestly admitted their own mistakes. We would find that we are not so different after all. We all make mistakes. In fact, we all make the same mistakes and that means we all have the same solution. If we could understand this, even to a minor degree, we wouldn't feel so alone. The goal for today: Practice humility ... find our similarities ... learn the common solution and see what human solidarity really feels like! Have a great day, everybody!

OCTOBER 26

That's Just Crazy

Treating people poorly won't make them want to treat me well. In the past, when people weren't acting the way I wanted, I would treat them like garbage to teach them a lesson, with the hope that they would come around and treat me right. Well, that's just crazy! If someone said to me that I should treat people the way that I would want to be treated, I would agree, but I certainly wasn't living that way. The goal for today: Treat people Right ... because it's the Right thing to do! Have a great day, everybody!

＝

Earn Forgiveness

Most of us have done things that we are not proud of ... God knows I have. One of the biggest mistakes I made was believing that I did things that were unforgivable—but now I know better. If I am Honestly sorry for what I've done and Truly willing to correct my mistake, then I will be forgiven. So the only unforgivable sin is the one I'm not sorry for ... that I continue to commit. The goal for today: Admit my mistakes, work toward correcting them, and earn my forgiveness! Have a great day, everybody!

October 28

Any Lengths

Are you really willing to go to any lengths to solve your problems ... to help others solve their problems ... to earn your own Happiness, Peace and Freedom? Most of my life, the honest answer to that question would be a resounding "NO!" I would let the government fix it. I would let my family and friends fix it. But I was never willing to do what was required of me to fix my problems properly. The goal for today: Grab the reins ... be responsible ... earn what I get and live Free! Have a great day, everybody!

The Art of Paying Attention

With a few key pieces of information and the ability to listen, there is nothing that can't be known. I have been practicing the art of paying attention and I've learned a lot. I have listened to thousands of problems and from what I've seen and heard, our solutions are always contained within the stories we are telling about our problems. The goal for today: Pinpoint the keys. Listen carefully to myself and others. Find real solutions to real problems and experience real Peace! Have a great day, everybody!

OCTOBER 30

The Paradox of Giving

When my life was coming apart, I needed help. I found that help, put it into practice and turned my life around. Now, I put my effort into offering help to others that want it and need it. The secret to solving my problems is to help you solve yours. The solutions I offer you apply to me as well. The more time I spend helping you, the less time I spend drowning in my own problems. The goal for today: If I need a prayer or a helping hand or a moment of kindness and caring ... I should give one! Have a great day, everybody!

Never Give Up

I never give up on anybody, but it is equally as important to not give in to anybody. There is a very fine line between helping and enabling—it's a very delicate balance. Everybody—absolutely everybody—is capable of change and that's why I will never give up on anybody. There is no such thing as a lost cause. At the same time, I can't always help people the way *they* want me to help them. The goal for today: Learn how to properly help people ... know that change is always possible ... and never give up! Have a great day, everybody

November 1

I Was Wrong

I spent many years believing that I could do the wrong thing and somehow get the right result. I thought I could be selfish and happy. I thought I could be angry and loved. I thought I could be dishonest and trusted. I thought I could be afraid and free. I was wrong! Trying to get a positive out of a negative is kind of like trying to throw things up and keep them from coming back down. The goal for today: Know that if I want to be Happy, Loved, Trusted and Free ... I MUST be Selfless, Loving, Honest and Pure! Have a great day, everybody!

Always Good

"God never puts us through more than we can handle."

Actually, God never "puts us through" anything. All pain, suffering, misery and trouble, comes from self-will—not God's will. Everything that is of God is positive, productive and helpful. All the trials and tribulations that I thought God put me through, were actually me testing God and myself to see if my way would somehow work out better than God's way. The goal for today: Know that God's way is ALWAYS good! Have a great day, everybody!

NOVEMBER 3

It Doesn't Work

I was living life backwards. I thought health would bring happiness ... I thought companionship would bring security ... I thought everything going my way would bring peace. I have spent far too much time trying to feel good on the inside based on what was going on outside of me and it doesn't work. The goal for today: Let happiness contribute to health ... let security and confidence lead to companionship ... and let peace rule the day! Have a great day, everybody!

Subtle Insanity

We are all insane to a certain extent. We all do things that we know we shouldn't do, and we all fail to do things that we know we should do. Example: I know I should drink less soda and more water, but, for some reason, I refuse to do it. I say things like, "I need something with flavor." Oh, I see ... the taste is more important than the physical affect ... yeah, that sounds sane. The goal for today: Stop writing this subtle insanity off as normal or natural ... and start working toward correcting it! Have a great day, everybody!

November 5

Humility ... Forgiveness ... and Freedom

Imagine going anywhere you want or need to go without fear of who you might run into ... no anxiety ... no discomfort. That's freedom, and that level of freedom comes from humility. When I admit my mistakes and forgive yours, I begin to make friends of my would-be enemies. Abraham Lincoln once said, "Am I not destroying my enemies by making friends of them?" And that just makes sense to me now. The goal for today: Humility, Forgiveness and Freedom! Have a great day, everybody!

My Only Real Need Is to Help You

I have to know the Truth about you, in order to help you, and the only way to know the Truth about you is to pay attention to you, and the only way to pay attention to you, is to pay less attention to myself. I have to actually listen to you rather than nod my head, not really listening, while waiting for my turn to talk. The best way to not know the Truth, is to not really listen. The goal for today: Put your needs ahead of mine, because my only real need is to help you! Have a great day, everybody!

Filter

Some people have no filter. What's on their mind comes out of their mouth and that can piss people off. Others have such a filter that they never say anything and they sometimes get walked on and taken advantage of. We need to find the happy medium—the middle ground. The unfiltered lets a lot of bull seep through and the over-filtered keeps even the Truth from coming out. The goal for today: Set my filter to separate the True from the false and then speak my mind! Have a great day, everybody!

꜡

Ask Not

"Ask not what your country can do for you, but what you can do for your country." —John F. Kennedy

This is a Principle that applies to every aspect of life. Ask not what my co-workers can do for me, but what I can do for my co-workers. Ask not what my friends can do for me, but what I can do for my friends. Ask not what my family can do for me, but what I can do for my family. Ask not what God can do for me, but what I can do for God. The goal for today: Give rather than get! Have a great day, everybody!

November 9

Ask God ... Don't Tell God

The key to having our prayers answered is to ask for the Right things and be as genuine and sincere as we know how to be. Did you ever ask God for something and promise that you would change your behavior in return, knowing deep down that you couldn't live up to your end of the bargain? Me, too ... many, many times. I fix this problem by asking God what He wants me to do, rather than telling Him what I want Him to do. The goal for today: Do God's will and get what I need! Have a great day, everybody!

November 10

Give Only Good

I hear people say "You get what you give." It sounds cute but I never took it literally until now. If I give you companionship, then I have your companionship. If I give you my time, then I have your time. Every time I help people, they are helping me. When I forgive, I am forgiven. Sometimes I literally get what I give directly from that person, sometimes I get it back in some other way, but I ALWAYS get what I give. The goal for today: Give only good! Have a great day, everybody!

Thank, Honor, Love

The brave men and women that devote their lives to defending our Freedom should be honored! They should be honored all day, every day, in the hearts and minds of all Americans! But, this day in particular is set aside specifically for us to honor them and I don't want to miss out on that opportunity. Thank a vet, Honor a vet, Love a vet and do all of that by living like an American. The goal for today: Trust God, Love my neighbor, Live Free! Happy Veterans Day! Have a great day, everybody!

NOVEMBER 12

⇁

Upward

"Setbacks are not important as long as the general movement of our lives is upward." —Emmet Fox

We all have problems and that's OK. What's not OK is to not take the time and put the effort into learning how to properly cope with those problems. If people wrong me, I will not wrong them back. I will seek to give Love, rather than get Love. I will not make decisions based on selfishness and fear. The goal for today: Faith and Fortitude ... Strength and Sanity ... Patience and Tolerance ... Kindliness and Love! Have a great day, everybody!

NOVEMBER 13

Permanent Solution

When I needed help I found a person to help me. But the Great Paradox of life is that the way he helped me was by teaching me how to help others. Constantly having people around to help me is not the permanent solution to my problems. Solving my problems and then helping others solve theirs is the permanent solution. The more I NEED you to help me, the further I have strayed from the Truth. The goal for today: Get what I need by giving that out freely to others! Have a great day, everybody!

Help People Help Themselves

The amount of effort I put into helping people is directly related to the amount of effort people are willing to put into helping themselves. I was unwilling to help myself most of my life; I wanted you to do it for me and that NEVER worked. The desire to be a willing participant in my own problem solving will absolutely be the deciding factor in whether or not my problems actually get resolved. The goal for today: Don't ask others to do what I could and should do for myself! Have a great day, everybody!

November 15

Spot the Wolf

Beware of the wolf in sheep's clothing! There are many powerful speakers in this world, but I have come to the realization that many of them don't actually know what they are talking about. The next time someone says something that sounds really inspiring ... try to do what they inspired you to do. If they can't tell you how to do it ... the message is probably BS. The goal for today: Don't just inspire people to change their lives ... show them how! Have a great day, everybody!

Think With Your Head, Know With Your Heart

The things I learn in my head, come and go. It is just information. But once I know something in my heart, it becomes a fact ... and a permanent part of me. The thing I enjoy more than anything else in life is watching people's eyes light up when they have some sort of profound realization. Sometimes these eye-opening moments change people's lives ... their whole way of living and thinking! The goal for today: Help people take off their blinders and live again! Have a great day, everybody!

Right Motives Make for Easy Decisions

There are no hard decisions. What's hard is trying to keep track of my motives. The motive that underlies my actions is what dictates whether it's the Right thing to do or the wrong thing to do. So if I am struggling to find my answers ... it's probably because I'm trying to manipulate an outcome. The goal for today: Practice keeping tabs on my motives all day, every day and watch the decision-making process get easier and easier! Have a great day, everybody!

If I Expect You to Treat Me Right

"Those who deny freedom to others deserve it not for themselves." —Abraham Lincoln

This is another Principle that applies to every facet of life. If I don't free you from my anger, condemnation and lies ... then I can't be free of anger, condemnation and lies. If I Truly realize just how literal this "You get what you give" stuff really is, I will stop treating people poorly, while expecting them to treat me right. The goal for today: Patience, Tolerance, Kindliness and Love ... no matter what! Have a great day, everybody!

Inside of Myself

I used to think I'd be happy when the right people came into my life. The right girl ... the right friends ... the right contacts. Yet again I was mistaken. Once I found peace and happiness inside of myself, then the right people came into my life. If I'm miserable, happy people might come around temporarily ... but if I continue my misery, they will go away in order to protect their own happiness. The goal for today: Don't base my happiness on people ... let people come into my life based on my happiness! Have a great day, everybody!

Doubt—the Destroyer of Progress

The best way to not get anywhere in life is to keep telling myself that I'm not getting anywhere in life. If I tell myself I can't overcome depression ... then I can't. If I tell myself I can't be free of anger ... then I can't. If I tell myself there is no hope for me ... then there's not. It is absolutely vital that I stop saying "I can't," because there is no greater destroyer of progress than a negative attitude. The goal for today: Know that "I can"... and so can you! Have a great day, everybody!

Simply Try to Be

"Nobody's perfect" isn't a good enough reason to not try to be. I know the things I say sometimes sound like I expect people to be perfect or that I think I'm perfect, but neither of those is accurate. I don't expect people to be perfect ... but I do expect them to try. I'm certainly not perfect... but I do expect myself to try. The goal for today: Don't tell myself I can't be perfect and don't beat myself up when I'm not ... simply try to be! Have a great day, everybody!

Believe

Why didn't I believe in miracles ... because they weren't happening? Or was it my disbelief that kept them from happening? Is the absence of miracles proof that they don't exist ... or does that simply prove that we don't believe? A lack of faith never got me anywhere good, so I decided to try the opposite. Now I have a truckload of faith and an infinitely better life than I had before. Still not perfect, but definitely headed in the Right direction. The goal for today: Believe! Have a great day, everybody!

Dominion

"God has given us dominion over all things."
—Emmet Fox

I no longer allow other people to control my life. I have regained control of my thoughts, my feelings and my actions. If people lie to me, I can use the brains God gave me to decide whether or not I believe them. If people treat me poorly, I can choose exactly how I'm going to feel about it. And once I'm thinking and feeling right, my actions will take care of themselves. The goal for today: Think Love, feel Love, give Love! Have a great day, everybody!

Whatever It Takes

There is a very interesting Principle in life that reminds me that I can literally accomplish anything that I set my mind to. If I am determined enough ... nothing and no one can stop me from achieving my goals. Unfortunately, it works both ways. If I am unwilling to do what is required of me ... nothing and no one can force me to succeed. The goal for today: Make the decision to succeed at life and then do whatever it takes to achieve that success! Have a great day, everybody!

Free From Anger

It's impossible for me to be angry without harming someone. The problem is that I'm hurting a lot more than just the person I'm angry at. I'm hurting myself ... I'm hurting my family ... my friends ... my co-workers. If I'm angry, I can't be happy. And if I'm not happy, I'm hurting the people around me. Anger is always destructive and therefore never justifiable. The goal for today: Free myself and everybody else from my anger! Have a great day, everybody!

~

On the Insider

Material achievements mean nothing if I don't like who I am on the inside. If I'm lonely, anxious, depressed and sad; worse yet, if I'm selfish, resentful, dishonest and afraid— then that big promotion at work doesn't really mean much. It's time to stop saying "It's what's inside that matters" if I don't really believe it. The goal for today: Honestly and genuinely, believe and understand that being a good person on the inside is the ONLY thing that matters! Have a great day, everybody!

NOVEMBER 27

What Could Be More Important?

I am thankful to those who have helped me and those who have let me help them. Everyone will have their moments when they need help and everyone will have their opportunities to help others. I couldn't have turned my life around without help and I can't keep it turned around without giving that same help out freely to others. The goal for today: Be grateful for the Family of Humanity—because what could be more important than that! Have a great day, everybody!

It Can Happen

If just reading these messages inspires you, imagine how inspiring it might be to live them ... to actually put this stuff into practice in your daily life. Imagine a world where people actually live like this ... now *that's* inspiring! And this has become one of my favorite statements: Before I say "That will never happen" I should make sure that I am not the reason it will never happen. The goal for today: Live Right and encourage others to do the same, because this CAN happen! Have a great day, everybody!

Does It Work?

There are reasons people don't sleep at night. There are reasons people feel angry, lonely, anxious, depressed and exhausted. The strange part is, the reasons are never what we think and are rarely what smart people tell us. When someone knows the real reasons for our problems ... they offer solutions that actually work. The goal for today: Let "Does it work?" be the deciding factor in whether or not a solution or treatment is accurate! Have a great day everybody!

Opinions Don't Outweigh Facts

If I'm doing what I believe God would want me to do, does it really matter what anyone else thinks about it? Most of my life, I was so wrapped up in what everybody else thought about me that I literally let it keep me from doing what I knew in my heart was Right. We all have opinions in our heads and we all have facts in our hearts ... I need to listen to the Right One. The goal for today: Don't allow people's opinions to outweigh God's facts! Have a great day, everybody!

December 1

Look Beneath the Surface

I need to understand myself and others, and in order to do so, I have to look beneath the surface. I can see the fear that leads to trouble. I can see the Truth about my lies. I can see the selfishness behind my giving. I can see the real cause of my anger. But the most important thing that I can now see is the solution to these problems. The goal for today: Find the Truth, apply the solution, help others do the same, and see what Happiness, Peace and Freedom really feel like! Have a great day, everybody!

DECEMBER 2

The Simple Science of Life

There is a science to life! Fear is the underlying cause of all my problems. If I don't work toward correcting that fear, it causes me to lie to myself. If I don't learn how to be honest with myself, it manifests into selfishness. If I don't try to fix my selfishness, it ultimately results in resentment and resentment is incredibly destructive. The goal for today: Seek and find the science behind our failure and success in life and the question "Why is this happening to me?" will be easily answered! Have a great day, everybody!

December 3

Permanent Happiness

There is a Right way and a wrong way to live. It's one thing to "get it," but it's entirely another to "give it." I'm always happy for people when they are able to turn their lives around, but I am supremely happy for those that help other people turn their lives around. Helping others is what will cement our own Happiness into place ... permanently. The goal for today: Help others the Right way, for the Right reasons, because altruism is the source of Happiness! Have a great day, everybody!

DECEMBER 4

Over-Compensation

When I'm living the Right way, I'm confident yet humble. When I'm living the wrong way, I'm arrogant yet unsure. It's strange how my fear, uncertainty and confusion come out sideways and look like arrogance, pomp and self-righteousness. Why is it that when I'm afraid I'm not smart enough, I act like a know it all? It's classic over-compensation and it needs to be corrected. The goal for today: Know that admitting I don't know it all is much better than pretending that I do! Have a great day, everybody!

December 5

And Move On

Panicking about my problems isn't going to fix them ... neither is feeling bad about them ... and neither is ignoring them. If I have a problem, there is only one Right thing to do about it—fix it! The only time I should talk about my problems is when I am in search of a solution. Getting it off my chest, not taking action to correct it, will actually make it worse and give it even more power against me in the long run. The goal for today: No anxiety, no depression, no "ignorance is bliss" ... spot, admit, correct and move on! Have a great day, everybody!

December 6

Regain Control

I am a big fan of personal responsibility! I used to believe that everything was someone else's fault and the problem with that theory was that I had no control over my own life. Sure I didn't have to take the blame for the problems in my life, but at the same time, my happiness was in someone else's hands too. The goal for today: Be responsible and regain control of my life ... the good and the bad, because personal responsibility leads to personal freedom! Have a great day, everybody!

December 7

Treat People Well

If I treat people well, no matter how they are acting, one of two things will happen: they will either change, or stop coming around me. This benefits everyone. Those who want to change will appreciate that you can see the good in them. Those who don't want to change will feel uncomfortable and drift away. The willing will change and the unwilling will continue to suffer and ultimately become willing to change. The goal for today: Treat people well ... because it's always wrong to treat people poorly! Have a great day, everybody!

Ask

Every question that has ever been answered had to first be asked. I never asked questions because I was afraid that it made me look stupid ... but now I see the immense value of asking questions. When I offer to help someone, they ask and expect me to have or find answers to their questions. The really powerful part of this is that I can't know how to help them if they don't ask questions. The goal for today: Ask ... because none of us can learn anything if we don't! Have a great day, everybody!

December 9

Base Elements

I thought fear would keep me safe, but doing the Right thing for the Right reason is where real Security comes from. I thought lying would keep me from being hurt, or hurting others, but the Truth is the only way to avoid pain. I thought helping myself would bring Happiness, but helping others is vital to Happiness. I thought anger and resentment were normal and natural, but Love and Peace are the true base elements of Human Nature. The goal for today: Live Right and Love Right! Have a great day, everybody!

DECEMBER 10

You're Not Alone

Somehow I convinced myself that everybody but me was supremely happy ... financially stable... highly intelligent... and just generally flawless. I'm not sure how I came to that conclusion, but I'm glad that I can now see the Truth. Everybody makes mistakes. Everybody has problems. I wasn't just dealt a bad hand—it's not just me. The goal for today: Admit my mistakes so other people don't have to feel so alone in this troubled world! Have a great day, everybody!

DECEMBER 11

What's More Important

Dr. Robert Smith once gave his medical services to five thousand men and women without thought of charge. Abraham Lincoln (a lawyer) once said, "Discourage litigation. Persuade your neighbors to compromise whenever you can." These two examples are a testament to how it used to be and how it should still be. Neither of these men went out of business ... neither of them went broke. The goal for today and every day: Make humanity more important than money! Have a great day, everybody!

DECEMBER 12

What We Do for Others

"One of the secrets of life is that all that is really worth the doing is what we do for others."
—Lewis Carroll

I love quotes like this that remind me of the vital importance of Loving my neighbor ... of having a genuine concern for the welfare of others ... of giving freely of myself so that others can live and be happy. The goal for today: Know that the reason we exist is to be Happy as a direct result of learning how to Love each other! Have a great day, everybody!

December 13

One Person Can Make a Difference

When you help people, you aren't just helping them, you are helping everyone that they come in contact with as well. I helped a friend from a town near home and she helped someone on the west coast and that person is helping people near him and those people are helping others ... and on and on. "Pay it forward" used to sound cute, but now that it's actually happening, I'm blown away! The goal for today: Pay it forward ... because one person can make a difference! Have a great day, everybody!

Love and Service Transcend

The more I thought about yesterday's message, the more the bigger picture came into view. The person that I helped was a white woman. The person she helped was a black man. He helped a Hispanic man and he helped a white man. This helped me see that there is a more important message here and that message is that Love and Service transcend all of the boundaries of gender bias, racism or religious dispute. The goal for today: Know that Love really does conquer all! Have a great day, everybody!

Move the World

"Give me a lever long enough and a fulcrum on which to place it, and I shall move the world."
—Archimedes

We human beings are the lever ... and God is our fulcrum. The more human beings that we can band together in unity, the longer the lever. Unity is brought about by knowing that God is our real strength ... our boundless support. The goal for today: Trust in God and Love my neighbor, because that's how I help move the world! Have a great day, everybody!

DECEMBER 16

Visionary

A Visionary is one who has Hindsight, Insight. and Foresight. If we look back in our pasts we can find many things that worked and many things that did not. A little bit of insight can show me whether or not what I'm currently doing is working. Then, with some foresight, I can form a rock-solid idea of what I should and shouldn't do moving forward. The goal for today: If life isn't working for me, I'll look back to find out why and do the opposite of that moving forward! Have a great day, everybody!

December 17

Heart ... Mind ... Eyes

Open my Heart, my mind and my eyes. When I open my Heart that makes it possible for me to believe things that were once impossible to believe. When I open my mind, I can properly process the information coming from my Heart to ensure that I won't be blindly led. Once my eyes are open, then I can clearly see the difference between the True and the false and then proceed to CHOOSE which one I will live by. The goal for today: Spiritual ... mental ... physical ... in that order! Have a great day, everybody!

True Strength

Is admitting that I've been hurt a weakness, or is my real weakness the fear that keeps me from admitting it? Not only does fear cause all of my problems, but it also keeps me from helping you solve yours. The two best reasons for me to admit my fears are: 1) I can't fix a problem that I refuse to admit exists. 2) Admitting them to each other, we can work together to solve our problems. The goal for today: Know that True Strength comes from admitting and overcoming my fears! Have a great day, everybody!

December 19

Unity

"We are people who normally would not mix. But there exists among us a fellowship, a friendliness, and an understanding which is indescribably wonderful."

That's what unconditional Love feels like! That's what the Fatherhood of God and the Brotherhood of man looks like! That is exactly how things ought to be ... and exactly how they are going to be in my life today! The goal for today: Love everyone, everywhere, in every way, because it's the Right thing to do! Have a great day, everybody!

DECEMBER 20

*

Quite the Contrary

How you treat me is not going to influence how I treat you. Quite the contrary ... how I treat you will dictate how you treat me. I will treat you with patience, tolerance, kindliness and love. What I won't do is let you walk all over me ... push me around ... take advantage of me or take me for granted. I will give and get exactly what I choose for myself today. The goal for today: Be kind and loving toward all without making a doormat of myself! Have a great day, everybody!

DECEMBER 21

The True Test

How you treat me is not going to influence how I treat you. Quite the contrary ... how I treat you will dictate how you treat me. I will treat you with patience, tolerance, kindliness and love. What I won't do is let you walk all over me ... push me around ... take advantage of me or take me for granted. I will give and get exactly what I choose for myself today. The goal for today: Be kind and loving toward all without making a doormat of myself! Have a great day, everybody!

DECEMBER 22

Rest ... Think ... Act

There's a time to rest. We either sleep or simply unwind to renew our minds. There's a time to think. We plan, schedule or contemplate, to get our minds Right before we take action. There's a time to act. With adequate rest, the mind can function efficiently and effectively and it becomes easy to see what the Right action is. When I don't rest, my thoughts are scattered and nothing seems to go my way. The goal for today: Rest, think and act ... then things will turn out Right! Have a great day, everybody!

DECEMBER 23

Unveil Your Heart

"The veil is still over their hearts." —2 Cor 3:15

We see things with our eyes, but we perceive things with our hearts. What the hell does that mean? My eyes told me that you were being mean to me for no good reason and I took it personally. My heart told me that you were in pain and you took it out on me because you didn't know what else to do. The goal for today: Remove the veil, see the Truth with my heart, and spread Love and Understanding around to everyone! Have a great day, everybody!

December 24

And Then ... Fix Them!

Someone recently asked me how I overcame a particularly difficult problem. I told her that I got so tired of listening to myself complain about it that I finally became willing to DO something about it. In fact, I became willing to go to any extreme necessary to not have to feel that way anymore. The goal for today: Don't evade. Stand toe to toe with my problems until they become completely unacceptable and then fix them! Have a great day, everybody!

DECEMBER 25

~

Always Right

If life is troublesome, I help others. If life is not troublesome, I help others. A fitting reminder in this, the season of giving. Helping others is the most important thing that I can do and I should do it frequently. Holidays are a reminder to be Loving and Giving, but it has to carry over into all times of year and in all of my affairs. The goal for today: Give freely of myself to others—not because it's Christmas, but because it is always the Right thing to do! Merry Christmas! Have a great day, everybody!

Headache ... or Heartache?

Sometimes I took medicine for temporary relief of physical ailments, but other times I took it because I didn't know any other way to get rid of emotional pain. Physical ailments can be treated and corrected medicinally, but emotional wounds cannot be. The fact is that a pill can fix a headache, but it can't fix a heartache! The goal for today: Fix physical problems physically, emotional problems emotionally, and mental problems mentally! Have a great day, everybody!

DECEMBER 27

~

Don't Live With It—Fix It

I frequently hear people talking about learning how to "live with" their mental illness. Well, the fact of the matter is that most mental illness can be overcome—we don't have to 'live with it'. Some mental illness is chromosomal and some is caused by a physical brain injury, but the chemical imbalance type of mental illness can be permanently eradicated by a process that is not always easy to practice, but is very simple in form. The goal for today: Don't live with it—fix it! Have a great day, everybody!

DECEMBER 28

Unselfish ... and Full of Faith

"When you find yourself in difficulties, you should pray for harmony and freedom, and expect to get it." —Emmet Fox

I used to pray and nothing happened, so I stopped. What I failed to realize was that I had no faith. I didn't believe that the prayers were going to be answered. This lack of faith, coupled with confusion about how to pray, kept my prayers from being answered. The goal for today: If I want my prayers answered, I must stop praying selfishly and start having faith! Have a great day everybody!

December 29

Unselfishness Abounds

I can't be understanding and angry. I can't care for others while thinking only of myself. I can't see the truth when I'm blinded by fear. And fear is the choice that sends me down this wrong path to begin with. When fear is the motivating factor behind my thinking, selfishness abounds and resentment is the end result. When Purity is the motivating factor behind my thinking, unselfishness abounds and Love is the end result. The goal for today: Purity, Honesty, Selflessness and Love! Have a great day, everybody!

DECEMBER 30

Live Free

I've come to the realization that the only time I can be lied to is when I don't want to know the Truth. The Truth about everyone and everything exists deep down inside of each and every one of us. If I am misled, I shouldn't get upset with the person that lied to me—I should get upset with myself for not using my intuition to see through it. The goal for today: Want the Truth ... seek the Truth ... know the Truth ... and live Free! Have a great day, everybody!

The Truth Motivates

Last night I thought to myself, *I need some sort of motivation to take better care of myself.* My next thought was, *It's silly to believe that I need some sort of motivation other than ... it's the Right thing to do.* Using outside props and false ideas might cause me to get up off my couch, but not for long. Doing the Right thing for the Right reason will always bring about more real and lasting results. The goal for today: Let the Truth be the only motivation I need today! Have a great day, everybody!

jeffreysbrown.com

Follow me on Facebook @ "Inspiration With Explanation" to receive up to date information about upcoming books and other projects.

For product information or questions regarding my writing, email me at

JSBrown625@gmail.com

If you are interested in writing me, mail can be sent to:

Jewelcor Bldg.
Room 130 (attn: JS Brown)
100 North Wilkes Barre Blvd.
Wilkes Barre, PA 18702

NOTE: Quotes that don't give direct credit to a specific author can be attributed to Alcoholics Anonymous.